UNLOCKED

A COLLECTION OF SIXTEEN SHORT STORIES

THE D20 AUTHORS

CONTENTS

FOREWORD

In November 2018, having been writing for nearly ten years, I finally did it: I signed a deal with publishers HQ/HarperCollins for my debut novel, *Little White Lies*.

The next year or so was a heady whirl of edits, cover design, marketing plans and early reviews. Feeling somewhat terrified during this rollercoaster period, I started to tentatively make links with other writers in a similar position: debut authors with their first ever books releasing in the year 2020.

Bit by bit, we shared hopes, fears and titbits of information as our books were prepared for publication. The common theme throughout these discussions was how excited and proud we were to be finally publishing the books we had, in most cases, been working on for years.

As our various publication dates drew closer, we daydreamed of seeing our books on the shelves in Waterstones, of reading our favourite passages aloud at author events, of meeting our readers, signing their books, and sharing the joy of it all with friends and family.

Then, Covid hit.

Writing and publishing a book is a hard task at the best of times. Being a debut author during what turned out to be almost two years of global lockdown didn't make things easier. Nobody was visiting bookshops. Nobody was hosting launch parties. Most people weren't even leaving the house.

I would never recommend launching your first book (or probably any book) during a global pandemic. However, the silver lining of all this was that out of the anxiety, isolation and uncertainty, our cohort of debut authors rallied together as a firm network of support and encouragement.

Formalised by the indomitable Polly Crosby as the Debut 20 group on Facebook, our network of over seventy authors has ever since been an incredible source of inspiration, cheerleading, laughter, tears and friendship. Over the last three years we have continued to share the highs and lows as we have gone on to write and publish our second, third and – in some cases – fourth or fifth books.

Along the way, we have also launched various profiles and projects. We have a thriving Twitter account (@TheD20Authors), expertly managed by Catherine Cooper, Kirsten Hesketh, Nicola Gill, Susan Allott and Louise Hare. Emma Christie created the brilliant Facebook events Diary of a Debut Novelist and Dictionary of a Debut Novelist. We have featured in news articles, podcasts and blogs, and taken part in panels at literary festivals (both online and in person, once that was again possible).

And we have produced this short story collection.

This ambitious project was born of my personal desire to highlight and celebrate the huge writing talent we have within our special group. I perpetually want to shout from the rooftops about the talent of my fellow D20 Authors (and I do shout regularly about them on Twitter). But what better way, I thought, to showcase the wonderful variety, originality and depth of the writers in our cohort than to compile and share such an anthology with you.

Not every author in our group has a short story in this book. However, I hope this anthology will act as a calling card for all of us, and that from dipping into the pieces in this collection you will be inspired to track down more of the brilliant stories D20 Authors have written and published. (To help you out, we have even collected all of our published books to date in one handy place: uk.bookshop.org/ shop/TheD20Authors).

I would like to thank all the authors who contributed a story to this collection. I hugely appreciate the time and work they have each given to this project. You will find more details about each writer at the end of their individual story – do check out their books via the links provided (or at the very least go and say hello to them on social media; they will be delighted to hear from you).

I would like to thank Caroline Bishop for her incredible work on proofreading this collection (including pointing out to me that this intro is a 'foreword', not a 'forward'). Also huge thanks to Charlotte Levin, Polly Crosby and Tom Benjamin who did such fantastic work on the cover design, and to Emma Bailey for bringing this all together in the beautiful image you see on the front of this book. Thanks, too, to Gina Wynn (ginawriteswords.com) who helped us with the formatting for publication. We are also hugely grateful to our promotions team: Debra Barnes, Emma Christie, Anna Jefferson, Tim Ewins, Gillian Harvey and Catherine Cooper.

Probably most importantly, we are delighted to be donating all profits to the Trussell Trust (trusselltrust.org). They support a nationwide network of food banks and together they provide emergency food and support to people locked in poverty, and campaign for change to end the need for food banks in the UK. We are honoured to be supporting them.

Finally, thank *you* for picking up and reading this collection. I really do hope you enjoy it.

Philippa East
October 2022

THE CLEANER

LOUISE MUMFORD

I love my job.

Noble profession, cleaning. You take the chaos and mess of people's lives, the smears and stains and overflowing bins, and you create order from it – you show them the gleam that lies underneath. You show them the *potential*.

Of course, then they mess it up again.

Some people might think this new job of mine weird, I guess. After all, I'm still working in the same building, on the same floor – in fact, I can even see my old desk. Nine to five, five days a week, twenty years: Mr Dedicott's Personal Assistant. Sounds fancier than it was, but I didn't mind that – I'm not fancy.

It was a big change, leaving. If I had my time again, would I have done anything different? Of course, yes. But things are what they are. I can't change them.

I'm here for a reason.

And it's not because of my love for emptying bins.

We work the night shift, which suits me. I'm not so good in the day anymore; I feel a bit fuzzy around the edges, floating from one place to another in a daze half the time. It's taken me a while to settle in. I don't mean in terms of banter and swapping trashy gossip mags with the others, I mean the effort of it. It's hard work. Hoovering, wiping, lifting, moving, bleaching. The concentration. No wonder I'm a wreck in the daytime.

I always do my desk first. No, not my desk anymore, I have to remember that. His. They replaced me with a man. Just a lad, I saw him the one time, skinny legs in those terrible tight suit trousers which young men wear nowadays, the kind that look as if they cut off circulation to the brain. I'm sure he's competent at his job.

But he's not me.

I was 'a treasure' Mr Dedicott said, more than once. 'What would I do without you, Miss Meriam?' he would say, and I would try to get him to call me Linda, but he wouldn't, not ever. He's a gentleman, Mr Dedicott.

I move the hoover over to my desk. I'm on my own. This is my floor. Always has been. When I first got the job, all those years back, I thought the building one of the swankiest I'd ever seen, even though only a little bit of it was Dedicott's. A little bit of something amazing was good enough for me.

I wish I could get the vacuum nozzle around the edges of the desk, but that skill is a bit beyond me just yet. Sign of a conscientious cleaner, nozzling. You'd be surprised how many of them here don't bother. On one side of the office there is a complete wall of glass, a bugger to keep clean obviously, but I look out across the twinkling city and wonder if anyone looks in … and, if they do, I wonder what they see.

I shouldn't dawdle. I never get more than an hour or so.

My desk was pristine. A place for everything and everything in its place. This was my place. *Is*. It still is. Mr Skinny Trousers doesn't quite have my flair for organisation. I wipe the surfaces and line up the paper and pens at neat right angles, brushing crumbs from the keyboard and emptying the bin of its chewing gum wrappers, drink cans and soggy bits of sandwich box.

I never ate lunch at my desk. Unhygienic. A good worker should never need to. You get your work done promptly, no messing around, and then you take your lunch break away from your work station. Get a bit of fresh air. Mr Dedicott agreed with me. Our times sharing a packet of crisps and reading our respective newspapers on a bench in the nearby park are some of the happiest of my life.

If it wasn't so dark, I would be able to see that bench from this window.

I never married. No children. I didn't choose it, but I guess, looking at it now, I didn't do much to stop it either. My mother would tell me to go out more, meet a nice man, let my hair down but, well … my hair stayed up, didn't it?

And I guess I did meet a nice man.

I'm struggling with door handles a bit at the moment, but I concentrate hard and finally the door opens into Mr Dedicott's office. I can't smell it anymore, but I know what the smell is: soap and leather and a thick layer of polish on old wood. A place for everything and everything in its place. I dust the framed photographs: grown-up child, wife. Her hair is long and waved in that way that looks natural but isn't.

She let her hair down.

What do I remember of my last day in work? At first, I couldn't recall much at all, but that's how the brain works, isn't it? Distressing images. It's like one of those parental controls on the television, it only allows you to see what is suitable. At least for a while. In the end, it came back to me.

I spent my morning as normal. The first thing I did when I came in was make sure Mr Dedicott's office was set up appropriately because the cleaners never got it right. Notebook and pen in their proper place, blinds half drawn, diary open to the correct page to show him the day's schedule, water jug filled, drinking glasses smudge-free. Then I settled into my computer work and fetched a cup of coffee for Mr Dedicott at 10.30am with accompanying biscuit or, when he was trying to tighten his belt, a banana. A snack at the desk is allowable, as long as it doesn't cause too much mess. I signed a birthday card for a slip of a girl I barely knew who could only have been turning twelve.

Lunch.

That was my mistake.

I was trying to be fancy. Trying to impress. Mr Dedicott always had such intricate lunches packed by his wife: a plastic box filled with smaller servings of salad and pasta in sauces I couldn't recognise. Branching out from my Tesco sandwich and meal deal, I went to one of those trendy deli-style cafes and got a mezze plate as a treat for us to share. Cuts of meat, some sweaty looking cheeses, hummus.

I died choking on an olive.

I can tell you it is not a pleasant way to go, not at all.

And then I was here. I don't know why I am, though I vaguely remember reading one of those trashy teen horror books when I was young, one about a ghost girl who had unfinished business and that's why she stuck around. But I didn't have any business to finish. After all, I died with my hair up. There aren't many others like me around. I thought

I'd found one a few weeks ago but it turned out to be one of the web development guys: a pale, floppy-looking thing. You can understand my mistake.

But you have to see the positives. I do. I can move things, at least. Every night I straighten Mr Dedicott's notebooks, make sure his cushions are plumped and leave his biscuit and banana ready for 10.30am the next morning.

I'm still useful.

I drag my vacuum out of his office and make my way back to where I left the cleaning trolley. I thought she'd be awake by now but no, as I move nearer, I see that she's still slumped in the chair in the corner. Jade, her name badge says. She's young, limp hair and huge hollow eyes. I'm not sure she's worked out that we have an understanding, but I know that every night she is grateful to sink into that chair and rest her head against the wall. 'Just a few minutes,' she mutters, and I like to think she is talking to me.

When she wakes up, most of the work has been done for her.

Noble profession, cleaning.

I love my job.

LOUISE MUMFORD'S DEBUT NOVEL, *Sleepless*, a 'frighteningly inventive' thriller inspired by her own insomnia, was published in December 2020 by HQ HarperCollins. A UK Amazon Kindle Top 50 bestseller, it was the Asda Karin Slaughter Killer Read for July 2021. Her second thriller, *The Safe House*, was published in May 2022. She is Co-Chair of Crime Cymru and part of the group bringing Wales's first crime fiction festival to Aberystwyth in 2023 called Gŵyl Crime Fiction Festival.

louisemumfordauthor.com

Twitter: @louise_mumford

Instagram: @louisemumfordauthor

Facebook: @louisemumfordauthor

MY LAST DUCHESS

CATHERINE COOPER

The temperature dips as soon as I step inside the thick walls of the chateau, away from the blistering heat of the sun. Since I arrived in France I've driven past many chateaux – some beautifully restored and almost perfect in every way, others dilapidated and tumbledown but still retaining a hint of their former glory. But this is the first time I've been inside one that isn't open to the general public. This chateau is neither pristine nor a near ruin but somewhere between the two – lived in, but not perfect.

'Thank you for coming, Laura,' the man says as he closes the door behind me. He is smartly dressed but non-descript looking – aged around fifty or so. 'Will you come with me to the studio please? Then we can get started. I don't like to waste time unnecessarily.'

Female sitter with long brown hair needed by artist. No nudity. Top rates paid, the advert on the local Facebook group for anglophones had said. Posted by someone called Robert with a profile image depicting a paintbrush.

I follow him along the flagstoned, bare-walled corridor, my shoes making a clack-clack sound which makes me self-conscious.

At the end we reach a large, light room with a wall of French doors overlooking a garden which has seen better days. The ceiling is high with a glittering chandelier hanging from the middle of an elaborate rose. In the centre of the shiny wooden floor is a wooden chair, and opposite it, an easel. One wall is almost entirely taken up with a painting of a woman in period dress – I'd guess from sometime around the 1800s.

Robert indicates a door in the corner of the room. 'If you go through there, you'll find the things I'd like you to wear for the sitting, please. And can you leave your hair down loose, like you did in the photo you sent me? Thank you. I will wait here.'

He turns away and starts fiddling with his easel and paints. I go into the next room where there is a tight-bodiced dress on a dressmaker's dummy, an elaborate hat with feathers on a stand and a ridiculously high-heeled, though admittedly beautiful, pair of boots laced with ribbons.

I remove the dress – which actually turns out to be a skirt and a top – from the dummy and find there's a large, hooped petticoat underneath. I assume I'm expected to wear that too and am thankful for the coolness inside the building. The top is lacy and off-the-shoulder, and the skirt is enormous and ruched at the base. They clearly aren't original – the top is stretchy so I can pull it on over my head and the skirt fastens with a zip, but they fit perfectly. As do the boots. I try and fail to remember if I sent my measurements.

I release my hair, put the hat on and look in the mirror. I smile. I look ridiculous, but somehow the outfit suits me.

It is tricky to walk in the boots as the leather is stiff and the heels are so high. I teeter over to the door, back into the room that Robert called the studio, and sit down at the chair. He is still fiddling with something on his easel and doesn't look up.

'I'll sit here, shall I?' I ask, already relieved to be off my feet.

He looks up. 'Thank you. Yes, please. If you could keep your back straight, angle your knees slightly toward the fireplace and direct your gaze at the other wall … Yes, that's it, like that. Thank you.'

Having positioned myself as he asked, it occurs to me I haven't asked exactly how long the job will take. The hourly rate was so exceptional I got overexcited and simply said yes before someone else snapped it up. This pose isn't the most comfortable of positions. I haven't found much work since I arrived in France from Ireland six months ago on a whim after splitting up with a boyfriend, so I could definitely use the money. I resolve to be as amenable as possible.

The room is silent but for the gentle splish-splish sound as he mixes colours on the palette and the rasp of his brush on the canvas.

I stare at the huge painting of the woman on the wall and realise that she's wearing exactly the same dress as I am now. She's also styled her long, dark hair the same way he asked me to, loose down my back.

Robert doesn't seem interested in conversation but after about thirty interminable minutes of silence I can't bear any more, so I venture, 'Who is the woman in the picture?'

He shrugs. 'No one. Just a sitter.'

We fall silent again. Because of the way he has asked me to angle my head I can't help but gaze at the painting. As I stare at it, I realise it's not just what she is wearing that is familiar, but also her face.

Perhaps she looks like me? Is that what it is? Maybe Robert has a type.

But as I continue to look, I realise it's not that after all. Her face is actually nothing like mine – much narrower, with a wider nose and fuller lips. I wonder which of us is better looking. Which of us does Robert think is more beautiful? Does he even care? Perhaps we are just bodies in a costume to him and he's not bothered about what we look like.

Given that I am wearing exactly the same dress as the woman in the painting, I imagine it is the costumes he is most interested in.

In spite of the chill in the chateau, I'm hot under my layers of skirts and my neck is stiff from the way I am twisting my head. But I don't want to complain, as he is paying so well that I definitely want to be asked back. The other painting is enormous – depending on his process, this could potentially be weeks of work for me. But at the same time, I could really do with a break to stretch out my aching body and maybe take the hat off for a while. I figure the best way to try asking for one is to start a conversation, even if he is unwilling.

'She looks familiar,' I say. 'What's her name? I think I've met her.'

He shrugs again. 'I don't remember. Lucy maybe. Something like that.'

We lapse into silence again as I continue to stare at the painting. The more I look, the more I see that she is nothing like me. But I recognise her. I'm sure I do.

I'm too hot, bored and aching and Robert is annoying me, excellent rate of pay or not. He hasn't even offered me a glass of water. I'm determined to continue the conversation so I can find a natural way to ask for the break that I'm sure I deserve by now.

'I'm sure I know her. Is she French? English?'

'Italian,' he says.

I feel a leap of joy as he engages in the conversation. It might have only been one word, but it's practically the first he's spoken to me that hasn't been an instruction.

'I couldn't help but notice I'm wearing the same dress as she is in the picture. Does the dress mean something to you? Or are you interested in the fashion of the period?'

He doesn't answer and carries on painting as if I haven't spoken.

I try a different tack. 'I like her smile. She looks friendly. What is she like?'

Robert sighs. 'A nice enough woman. Easily pleased. Maybe too easily pleased.'

I'm not sure what he means by that, but I don't ask. 'Does she not sit for you anymore?' I persist, wondering if she gave up because she was never offered a break.

'No. She had too many other things she wanted to do. And she talked too much,' he adds, pointedly.

As I continue to look at the painting I suddenly remember why she seems familiar. Her picture was in the paper and on the news. She went missing. A few weeks ago.

My face grows hot and a bead of sweat runs down my back. 'Other things? Like what?' I ask, trying to keep my voice steady. 'Where is she now?'

He sighs again. 'She's still here. But she's silent now. Shall we get on? I would so like another one just like her to add to my collection. I've locked the doors, in case you're wondering. Now could you please turn your head back towards the wall? Thank you.'

CATHERINE COOPER IS a Sunday Times Bestseller and author of *The Chalet*, *The Chateau* and *The Cruise*. She lives in the South of France with her family.

catherinecooperauthor.com

THE REEF

EMMA CHRISTIE

Now, her breath was everything.

She pictured her lungs, fat with life. The muffled whisper of each inhale and exhale was amplified by the snorkel tube, made her feel bigger than she was.

But more guilty.

She sighed then swam through the sound of it, repeating one phrase in her head.

Alan made me do this.

She headed back to the boat, grunting as she pulled herself onto the narrow metal steps hung over the side. She wanted to reach for Alan's chaffed hands, feel them grip her freezing, slippery fingers. She wanted him to haul her over the side of the boat like a prize catch, to wrap her in an oversized towel and bring her the last of the whisky. Not this. Never this.

She had one foot on the top rung when the boat lurched to her side, throwing her back into the water. She tried again, fell again, then gave up. She'd swim for a while instead, watch life.

The sea was calm today. A few fish inspected the sandy floor, bellies flashing green and blue and silver when they turned and caught the light. Some swam alone, hunting and hunted. But mostly they moved together, stayed low and headed towards the reef. Towards Alan.

She started swimming after them, then hesitated and checked her watch. Grief clogged her throat. The worst part – the watching part – wouldn't be over yet. There would still be movement, traces of loss. No, she'd stay well away until Alan was definitely gone. She turned around and kicked hard, one arm stretched ahead of her as she powered through the water. She kept the other arm by her side, hand gripping the smooth handle of the harpoon gun.

Its blade was old but sharp. She'd cut her fingers on it dozens of times and she was sure Alan must have killed hundreds of fish with it over the years. One click and its sleek silver tip would zip through the blue, slice up a life in an instant. And death was always silent underwater.

She'd hung back the first time he used it, gazed down from the surface as he swooped downwards and snaked along behind a twitching fish with a black-tipped fin. She'd been surprised he could hold his breath for so long, but he'd persevered, followed it until he got the right angle to fire.

A blade through the head and it was dead.

Alan had told her later that he always aimed for the eye – mainly because it released less blood, but also so he could slip a wire through the puncture hole, string up his kill like a charm bracelet.

She'd vomited when he did that, pulled off her mask and spewed lumps of mushy cornflakes over the surface of the water. The fish had loved it. They'd swarmed around her, lips flapping as they gobbled up every soggy crumb of her breakfast. The sight of it had made her heave even more and Alan had laughed, too much.

Then he'd put the harpoon into her hands.

'It's easy,' he'd said, and she'd wanted to believe him. She'd loaded the gun, then started looking for a target, trailing shoals that moved like clouds over a wordless planet. Alan had tapped her arm when he spotted a lone fish, and she'd dived down, closed in on her prey as it nibbled a strand of dying sea grass. She'd taken aim, finger on the trigger – then took a deep breath by mistake and flooded her mouth with water. Alan hadn't helped her, just laughed again when she pushed her head above water, coughing and spitting and wishing she loved a more thoughtful man.

He always laughed at the wrong times – when he got bad news, when he saw someone fall over, when they were talking about money or work or analysing some stupid fight they'd had.

All of their fights were stupid, really. She'd always been surprised by the ferocity of their rage, wondering where it came from, where it went. But the most agonising part came later, once the shouting had stopped and they'd both said sorry. She'd look back at the words fired like bullets between them and she'd know – just know – that they'd meant every one of them. Maybe just for a moment, but that was enough.

The bitterness that came so easily to them both left a stain that neither could shift.

That was probably why he'd cheated.

It was definitely the reason she had.

Still, she'd always come back to him and their shabby house on the headland. And Alan always welcomed her home in the same way, saying storms made the sea even more beautiful.

She almost cried then, but fought it. She flipped onto her back, took off her mask and rubbed her eyes with wrinkly fingers. It made things worse. Sunlight and seawater seeped in, released a few of the tears she'd tried to push back inside. She cursed herself, then stared at the sky and drifted, listening to the gulp of waves and the screech of sea birds she'd never learned the name of.

The water pushed her round to face the bay, a curve of dirty grey sand backed by granite hills and mottled sky. It was the kind of place you'd drive past and never think of stopping – and even if you did stick around, you wouldn't take photographs.

But this was the beach they'd vowed to never leave. It was where they'd met, where they'd married, where they'd hoped to raise children.

It was theirs for life, Alan had said.

But he'd had no idea how soon that life would leave him.

She coughed suddenly, spat out water thrown up by a swell. Salt nipped her eyes as she fitted her mask and rolled onto her front, let the tide tug her away from the shore.

It was time to finish what she'd started.

Her mask steamed up when she put her face back into the water, but she kicked hard and kept going, knowing exactly where she was headed. The reef. It wasn't as impressive as it sounded, never had been. She'd seen some that were like underwater rainbows – vast, spindly coral filling the empty blue like leafless trees, neon branches sharp as cut glass. Others looked like giant brains, each thought and idea and memory throwing up a different colour. But this one was just a long rocky wall, a sprawling underwater garden that attracted fish and crabs instead of birds and mice.

Alan had fallen in love with it thirty years ago, when he was eight years old.

His dad had often dragged him and his big sister on fishing trips when they were too young to stay at home alone. They'd found it boring at first, just something else to whine and cry and fight about. It had all changed the day his sister thumped him so hard he fell over the side of the boat, eyes open, and saw a new world beneath him. After that, he'd always taken his swimming goggles, despite his dad's much-repeated warning. *You'll catch your death in that bloody water.*

Almost, she thought, almost.

She shivered as the seabed dipped away from her. Rocks dotted the sand, poking out from the rippled bed like moles on old sun-wrinkled skin. Some were smothered by spongy red moss, others sprouted long green leaves which seemed to sway in time with her breathing. She stopped, stilled her legs and moved herself in gentle circles using her free arm.

Fish the size of fingers poked at seaweed. A brown crab scuttled past. Red anemones pulsed.

She'd found it unnerving at first to find herself suddenly among them, a bony, hairy, clumsy part of this shimmering underwater world. She'd barely even paddled in the sea before she met Alan, held back by irrational childhood fears of deep water, fish with teeth and sinking.

Now she couldn't picture life without the sea, and them in it.

Alan never bothered testing the temperature before he hurled himself into the water, and always teased her when she trailed her hands over the side of the boat, wincing when the cold waves stung her fingers. *We're in Scotland*, he'd say, shaking his head.

She'd smile down at him from the edge of the boat, then close her eyes and let herself drop into the water beside him, always with a gasp she'd try to conceal but never could. She'd swear, he'd laugh, she'd laugh. Then they'd bite down on their mouthpieces and turn their faces into the water. In that instant, their breathing was all they could hear, and all that they wanted to.

Alan would always paddle ahead of her. He'd smacked her in the face with his flippers a few times but she'd soon learned to hold back, just follow the trail of tiny bubbles he left behind.

She'd also learned that fish didn't pay her any attention, even when she tried to scoop them up, grabbing at them with slow-motion fingers. They were always further away than they looked. Alan had taught her that too, and everything she knew about waves, tides, currents.

And harpoon fishing, of course.

She and Alan had come here the day he told her it was ending. He'd forced his voice to be strong until they were alone, made some joke about best-before dates as they headed for the car. Then he'd asked her one final favour. She'd nodded, agreed, felt broken.

They'd driven to the harbour in silence then taken the boat straight to the reef. Hoods up, heads down, waiting for the familiar slap of sea spray against their skin as they bumped over waves. Then they'd tossed in the anchor, sipped some burning whisky and wriggled into their wetsuits. For once, they'd plunged into the water together, then he'd taken her hand, led her.

They'd always swum with their fingers entwined in the early days, despite his complaint that swimming with one arm was far more tiring than swimming with two. He was right, but it had made her feel less alone in the vast sea. It had taken her a while to realise that was exactly the feeling Alan wanted when he was in the water. Total isolation from noise and touch and words. And later, from pain.

He'd tugged her arm when they reached the narrowest section of the reef, and they'd both brought their heads up, pushed their masks over their foreheads.

'Here,' he'd said, eyes down. 'It's got to be here.'

She'd nodded, gazed at the anonymous swells around her. 'But where should I—?'

'I'll show you,' he'd said. 'And don't even think about tossing me off the harbour. You hear me? I'd just be swallowed by a gull, end my days as sticky shit on a car windscreen. No, you're firing up the boat, bringing me here and taking me under. But just you, mind. Just you.'

They'd dived down, following the bumpy reef wall until Alan pointed to a small opening close to the sand. She'd peered in, not sure what she expected to find. It was narrow but long, and empty apart from tiny barnacles. She'd given him a thumbs up then started looking around, wondering how she'd remember the spot. But Alan had already thought of that. He'd tugged her arm again, then made her watch as he wedged his harpoon gun into the hole. It would stay there until she needed it.

And today was the day.

She'd found his harpoon as soon as she dived down – but couldn't pull it out. She'd gone up for air five times before she managed, resting her feet against the side of the reef and pushing off as hard as she could, both hands gripping the handle.

After that, she'd peered into the hole again to check it was empty.

Then filled it with little pieces of Alan.

A gritty cloud had made the blue turn grey when she loosened the lid, then she'd headed for the surface without looking back. This was what she'd promised to do, but she couldn't watch. Wouldn't.

Christ, she'd already seen the life drain out of him once.

There were only a few fish near the hole now, stragglers sucking in the last dots of ash. She smiled when a fat-lipped fish peeked out from the mouth of the urn, glared at her, then slipped back inside. Alan would have approved. She stopped kicking, hung above the reef and let her world become salt water.

The sea held her still.

EMMA CHRISTIE WAS BORN and raised in a book-filled house in Cumnock, an Ayrshire coal-mining town. After quitting her law degree to study literature and medieval history at Aberdeen University, she spent five years working as a news reporter with one of the UK's top-selling regional daily newspapers, The Press and Journal. Her debut novel *The Silent Daughter* was shortlisted for the McIlvanney Prize for Scottish Crime Book of the Year 2021, shortlisted for the Scottish Crime Debut of the Year 2021 and longlisted for the Crime Writers Association John Creasey (New Blood)

Dagger Award 2021. Her second novel, *Find Her First*, was published by Welbeck in Jan 2022.

emmachristiewriter.com

Twitter: @theemmachristie

Instagram: @theemmachristie

Facebook: @theemmachristie

WHILE THE HENS ROOST NIGHTLY

NIGHTLY

PHILIPPA EAST

The chicken is dead on the doorstep, one wing splayed, near pulled off. Its feet are tucked out of the way; its neck is broken, feathers gummed with blood. I gather my skirt about my knees and crouch down to press its breast with my palm. One eye stares at me, glazed over like a scuffed bead.

The other five hens are still in the birch trees. I hear them clucking to each other, making to settle themselves. I pull on my wellington boots and tie my hair up with a bandana. *You have to go slow next time, Annie*, I tell myself, *clean and tidy, like a good wife.* The feed pail in the porch is half-filled with grain – I'll have to empty that first – but here's my mackintosh on its usual peg, and my garden gloves, the scratchy cloth so familiar. I step over the crumpled hen and carry the pail of feed out to the yard. The puddles are iced over and there's hoarfrost dusting the fence posts. I fling the corn across the gravel, trying to whistle the way Jamie taught me, though the sound doesn't come out right, what with my lips so dry and cracked.

The chickens start up their flutter and coo among the branches as I rattle the pail, looking at each other with their orange eyes to see who'll jump first. I know they're hungry. I tip up the bucket and bang on it like a drum, and at last they cackle and fly down.

They stampede for the corn, strutting up my shins and scrabbling their sharp feet over the plastic of my boots. I stumble away, and they squawk and flap for purchase. I go back to the house with the empty bucket.

The dead hen fits the bottom of the bucket neatly, tucked up in its tin nest. It leaves some feathers behind, stuck to the stone step. I'll need to scrub that later. I carry the pail across the yard and past the kennel. At the end of the garden there's a pigsty, ramshackle and overgrown with nettles. The roof is curved and there's a low door to the side to let the pig in and out. There used to be a sow, but nothing lives in there now. I stamp down the nettles and squat in front of the doorway. The chicken wire across the front comes away easily enough. It's too dark to see but there's a cloying, earthy smell in there, like compost or dung.

I slip the feathery body inside. Then I put the chicken wire back.

OURS WAS a New Year's wedding bright with snow, a year ago, at the registry office in town. Father gave me away with a cough in his voice, and I wore blue and told Mother it was the happiest day of my life.

Jamie was pale as porridge oats in his dapper brown suit. His eyes were sad even though he was smiling; I thought that would grow better in time, but it never much did. He became a man young, did my Jamie. An orphan at twelve when a barn fire took his family, though who'd have thought it in this day and age? Twenty when we married, and I was barely nineteen but neither of us cared to wait around.

We bought the house with our savings, the money I'd put aside from my factory work in Galston. He had an inheritance too, though he balked to touch even a penny of it. We arrived there along with the snowdrops, with a removals truck and a suitcase each, and stood in the road looking at the place. It'd been sold off cheap, being so old-fashioned and far from town, but Jamie took my hand, with a shining in his eyes, and said, 'Here's where we'll build our home, Annie, here's where we'll raise our bairns.'

I caught the glow too and felt right enough that we would be happy there, that I could make him happy, good little wife that I'd be. So I made the place nice, putting up new drapes in all the rooms and scrubbing the old lino till it gleamed. It didn't take a day before it was covered in mud and paw prints again, but I tried.

We put about our pictures and furniture and hung his father's shotgun in pride of place above the mantlepiece. The dog came with us from Kilmarnock, and there was a pigsty in the garden so Jamie said we should get a little pig, and when the price of eggs went up that Easter he bought the half-dozen chickens too. I wasn't used to all the fluttering and snufflings; I worked in the canning factory where machines made all the noise. But I did my best to tend for the animals, because I knew Jamie cared for them and that's what mattered most.

⎯⎯⎯⎯

I FILL a bucket with soapy water and scour the doorstep on my hands and knees. The water quickly turns rusty from the dirt and blood and I pour it out in the yard, watching it soak down through the stones. I refill it from the kitchen tap and inch by inch I work my way backwards across the floors of the house, scrubbing away the marks and stains. The soap gets into the cuts on my hands, and my knees bruise against the floor, but under the sweep of the water, the old brown tiles come up good as new.

THOSE FIRST FEW months fair flew by, we were so busy making the place our own. We cleared out the fireplace and fixed up the lights where the wiring had worn through. Soon, the place was so warm and welcoming that even on the nights when foxes barked and it was black as pitch on the hill, we never felt but cosy and safe. The seeds I'd planted in the garden began to push up with all the April showers, and come May the lawn was specked with meadow flowers. I took to picking and pressing them and often fussed at it long into the evenings till Jamie called over the banisters saying it was late, wasn't I coming to bed?

'Why – can you no get warm without me?' I'd call back, though maybe I did stay up late on purpose some nights. Even in the daytime Jamie was always coming at me with kisses and cuddles and cow's eyes. And I don't mind a peck here and there, but the rest of it brought back something I didn't like; it bothered me the way he'd creep his hands onto me saying, 'Annie, Annie'. One night I told him so, and it came out sharper than I meant. Well, Jamie went quiet then and I knew I was mistaken for being so unkind. And I didn't hardly sleep that night, wondering why I should feel like that about my Jamie when I loved him so much and only wanted to make him happy.

The factory girls only smirked and rolled their eyes, so in the end I took my pride in my hands and went and spoke to Mother about it. Mother has a sharp face and a sharp tongue, and she keeps her thoughts to herself unless hard pressed.

'Mistakes are made, but mistakes can be mended,' was all she said. 'The sooner there's a bairn between you, the better.'

And Father said nothing at all, barely looked at me, just scraped his chair back from the table and banged the door behind him on his way out.

When I got home I busied myself cleaning the oven and putting out pellets for the mice I'd heard scrabbling, and when Jamie came in that evening I told him I was sorry and would do better in future. It didn't matter, he said, he loved me all the same. Only I ought to remember he was my husband and there was nothing wrong in it.

THE CHICKENS ARE WELL-FED and sleepy now. I watch them settle on the lawn. From the kitchen I take the carved wooden chairs – a wedding gift – and pile them up at the side of the kennel. I fill in the gaps with logs from the wood stack and the picture frames I took down yesterday. Upstairs, the bedstead and dresser are too heavy to move, so I leave them where they stand and cover them with dust sheets.

In the bedroom, I climb onto a chair to pull the suitcases down from the wardrobe. I take the clothes from the cupboards and drawers, packing them into the cases, mine and Jamie's. The last I put in is my blue wedding dress, the lace still as fresh and pretty as ever. I buckle the suitcases up and carry them down the narrow stairs, sliding one in front of me and dragging the other behind. I line them up next to each other in the hallway, near the door so they're ready and waiting for us, just like when we first arrived.

From the empty rooms, I unhook the curtains and carry them outside to add to the pile. The wood is damp and I have to empty a whole can of petrol over it before it will light, but then the cheap cotton drapes go up in a whoosh. The rising smoke fills the air, smudging up the gathering clouds.

———

WHEN THE EVENINGS GREW LONGER, Jamie and I would sit up talking our thoughts till the wee small hours. We drew the soft chairs together in the front room and I'd tuck my feet up in the cushions while Jamie tuned the radio. He always preferred the crackly, old-time songs, the tunes his parents listened to when he was a boy. While they played, he would talk in a way he never had before, like something was opening up in him as we settled into our lives here. Tales of the games he'd played with his sister and of his parents' gentle ways, and the happiness he knew in those years before the fire. When I listened to him, his happiness became mine too, taking me away from my own small childhood, cold and narrow and not worth thinking of. I could see what it was to be a family, living and laughing and loving together. I knew then that I was safe with Jamie, seeing the gladness in his eyes and feeling the new warmth that ran between us when he held my hand in the dark.

One day in the early summertime, I came home bone-tired from the early shift, but the sun was out and the garden in full bloom. I put on a patterned smock and Jamie spread a blanket on the strip of grass that stretched from the west of the house to the birch trees, and we lay on our backs staring up at the sky. I'd shut the chickens in the coop to stop them scratching up my peony seeds, and the dog and pig were asleep together like two old friends in the shade of the kennel.

Jamie lit up a cigarette and blew the smoke in blue curls over our heads.

'I would get a raise at the dairy,' he was saying, and I nodded my head to show I was listening. 'We could paint the room at the back, make it nice, and you could sew the curtains.'

'Blue or pink?' I heard myself ask.

Jamie laughed. 'We'll see.' He patted my hand. 'But if it was a girl we could call her Mhairi.'

That was the name of his sister that died in the fire. I kept quiet at that, just smoothed down my skirt where I felt it lift in the breeze. But it felt good to be making plans and it was what we both wanted, after all. He's a good man, I told myself. He'd make a good father.

Jamie went on talking and his voice blurred in with the noise of a car puttering by beyond the fence. Everything was so still and peaceful, I closed my eyes and let the sun warm me through. We lay that way for a bit, with Jamie blowing his cigarette smoke and me swimming in and out of a doze. Then I must have fallen right asleep because when I came round Jamie's hand was on me. I hadn't put a vest on and now my top buttons were undone. I held my eyes shut and kept breathing in and out.

His fingers rolled and squeezed on my breast, like the way he once showed me he'd milk a cow. *It's different*, I said to myself this time, *he's your husband, Annie, just let go*. His hand went on circling under my dress until his breath got a catch in it and he shifted closer on the blanket. Clouds had come over the sun and the air was cold without it. Little goosebumps stood up on my arm, turning the skin to plucked turkey. But he was quick about it, and afterwards I was glad I'd let him. He'd been patient with me all this time, and the next month we were so happy when I returned from the doctor with good news.

'I lost all my family, Annie,' he said, drawing me close, 'but we're starting a new one, together, you and me.'

THE HENS DON'T LAY any more. Perhaps it's the cold weather or perhaps they know we've no need for eggs now. At noon I catch another three, one after the other, neat and clean. I don't let myself think about it even as their necks twist under my hands. I'm careful this time, I don't tear at them like I did the first one in my anger. Three hens fill the pail up to the brim, one on top of the other, so tidy and still as I take them down to the bottom of the garden. The remains of the brood are cosied together in a corner of the yard, just two left now, tossing their heads at the rain spots coming down and shaking out their feathers.

Indoors, where it's warm still, I check off the list I've made. It's as if the days are running backwards now, like a full river flowing upstream.

On the back of the paper I write a letter to Mother, explaining everything.

———

SOON THE AUGUST days were shortening but the light in the evenings was still enough for me to hem the curtains by. We chose yellow in the end, as Jamie said yellow could work for laddies or lasses, and it was his sister's favourite colour. We hung the curtains in the nursery window and set the cot against the wall underneath. Those first two months I could barely look at a lettuce leaf without reeling; it never did settle, always felt like something was working loose somewhere, but Jamie said I was a trouper, and made me put my feet up on cushions while he cooked fresh omelettes from all the eggs the hens had laid.

At nine weeks I handed in my notice at the

factory. A shame, said Mr Gregory, he'd had his eye on me for a management position. When I got home that evening the house felt tighter, like the roof had hunkered down or the walls had shrunk in. I told Jamie I needed to rest awhile and went upstairs and sat in the new nursery. I cupped my hands over the bowl of my belly and pushed myself back and forth in the rocking chair.

The sky over the birches turned from gold to red as I sat and rocked. I thought of how the lines of family grow like tree branches, drawing water up from the roots, so that every bud and new leaf that blossoms on the twigs is watered in the silt of the generations come before. And that night I dreamt of veins in tree trunks, pumping mud and sticks and matted feathers.

At the end of the summer, the chickens puffed out their plumage and flapped one by one into the birch trees. The rain fell again and we took to closing the windows at night as the high September heat began to fade.

IN THE LEE of the kennel, I catch another hen, the second to last. I gather her into my arms and bury my face in her wings, feeling her heart scamper under my fingers. I hold her tight and she makes no sound as she goes.

———

WHEN THE CRAMPS TOOK HOLD, climbing home up the hill, I sensed at once what it was. I dropped my shopping bags right there in the lane, but I didn't make it further than the gate. The hill was too steep and it happened so quickly, and that's where Jamie found me, coming home from the dairy half an hour later, kneeling in a patchwork of blood.

Later, the doctor came and examined what was left and gave me pills to help me sleep, and a week or so went by that way. Some mornings I'd wake and think the baby was still in me, and other mornings I'd wake forgetting I'd ever been pregnant at all. Either way there was no child and when I saw the look on Jamie's face I was pricked with shame.

I told him I was sorry, and only wished he would say it didn't matter, that he loved me just the same. But instead his eyes went like hollows above his cheeks and he passed his hand again and again across his face. I know he tried his best to be kind but it was like a raging devil had got inside him, like the storm clouds that come over a man when he's in drink. In the nights he'd toss and turn, jolting awake with sweat pouring off his brow shouting, 'Mhairi! Mhairi!' Many's the time I wanted to reach across and pull his head down on my chest and hold him there to soothe us both. But I was frightened and frozen inside and all I could do was say, 'Don't think of it, that fire's been and done, go back to sleep'. Then he'd turn away, stiff as a board, or else go outside and stand in the yard. I could see him from the window, staring into the birch tops, patting the pig he'd grown fond of and watching the chickens sleep there in the trees.

Come November, Mr Gregory wrote to say my old job was still there if I wanted it. I couldn't think what else to do so I went back to work. It felt better to be out of the house, away from the silence and the empty cot in the nursery. It seemed the space was good for Jamie too. He never said out loud, but it felt like he'd made up his mind to put the torments behind him now.

And so I believed that we'd draw close again, come tip-toeing back to each other, in the shortening days up there on the hill.

I LIFT the key from its hook in the hall and pull the door hard shut behind me. The lock is stiff but I manage it with both hands. Now the house is shut up tight. The key goes into my mackintosh pocket, ready and waiting for when we return. Inside, in the kitchen, the telephone is ringing, but there's no need to answer that now. Outside, despite the cold, the fire I made is burning steady.

ON CHRISTMAS DAY, I saw him as I came down the stairs, his back to me in the open doorway, cold air seeping in. Almost a year it was since we'd married, though you'd hardly think it to look at us.

I came down a step closer. 'Where're you going, Jamie?'

I saw his shoulders jerk, and I came down another two.

'Where're you going?'

I saw his hand come up to wipe his eyes, to remove the wet, as if I didn't already know he was crying. I wiped my own fingers on my pinny because I was close enough now to touch him, to lay a hand upon his shoulder. Close enough to lead him back inside and cross the long distance between us.

'Where're you going, Jamie, with your father's gun?'

He drew a breath. His shoulders rose and his back straightened and he hoisted the shotgun under his armpit. He didn't look round at me, his wife, standing there in the hallway.

'To kill the pig,' he said.

And it was such a surprise all I could think to say was, 'Be sure to get a clean shot then.'

From the kitchen window I could see the yard, still covered with rime that hadn't thawed all morning. I watched Jamie walk past the kennels and disappear around the corner, headed for the pigsty at the end of the garden. I turned the turkey in the oven and weighed out the flour for the bread sauce. I ran scalding water in the sink and over my hands until I couldn't feel the pain of it anymore. It was so quiet, inside the house and out.

THE CHICKEN IS HOPPING and flapping round the yard and my wellington boots come stomping after it, sliding in the wet gravel. I can hardly see for the drenching rain but I've got my hands outstretched to catch it, the last one. The hen is squawking and I'm weeping too, because this one was his favourite, white all over with the longest neck of them all.

I HEARD the shot all right. I heard the shot and a chill went through me. I told myself, that's the sow gone for good, but even then I knew it was a lie. I pretended I should go out and help him with the carcass, though I hadn't the first idea what we'd do with it. I supposed Jamie would know, having grown up on a farm and being brought up that way.

I pretended for a long time, standing in the kitchen up to my elbows in the sink, waiting for Jamie to come back through the door.

And then I saw the sow waddle out from behind the dog kennel.

I felt like laughing. I felt like rolling around the floor and beating my face and tearing out my hair as I stood and stared at the pig trotting up the yard with its curl of tail in the air.

I remember drying my hands on my skirts and walking outside without even stopping to put shoes on. I walked out into the yard; the cold bit into my bare feet and the gravel lodged under my toenails. The chickens came crowding round, grubbing for food and pecking my toes. I walked past the kennel where the pig liked to live, where she'd always liked to live. I kept walking and the wind was blowing as if trying to hold me off, push me back into the warm house. But I walked on with my mouth open, and the cold air went through me like I was a ghost.

When I got to him he was lying face down, and there was a tangle at the top of his head, like some messy, ragged hat, dark and shiny. The shotgun was underneath him; he'd fallen forwards onto it, flattening the nettles in front of the sty like he'd tried to beat a path to the doorway with the weight of his body. And all I could think of was to mend it then and there. I said to myself, *Jamie came out here to kill the sow, that's what he said*. It was a simple mistake, and mistakes could always be mended. So I took the shotgun, tugged it out from under his belly and checked there was a bullet still left in the chamber.

Our pig was standing in the shelter of the kennel, with the dog sitting next to her looking at me with his eyes full of questions. I did it quickly straight between the ears and the dog leapt away in fright at the bang. The sow just knelt down onto the ground and rolled over and twitched its legs and then lay still, its tail uncurling and hanging down, so I knew it was dead just as Jamie had meant it to be. It was hard work to drag her down to the pigsty, but I did it. I pushed them both in through the low door and put chicken wire over the hole, tucking them away out of the cold, out of sight, out of mind.

For three days straight the dog howled and

wouldn't stop, turning its teeth up to the moon and baying fit to burst. He went on and on though I scolded him and smacked his nose. I clapped the pillow over my ears but still I could hear it, and the chickens outside were crowing away, too, in their fear. I pressed my fists into my cheeks.

Come the fourth day, I took the tin from the cupboard under the sink. I poured the pellets out into the bowl and mixed them with canned meat, and put a bowl of water out, too, beside the kennel. Soon I heard barking, then the skittering of the gravel as he dashed round in circles. Then a keening noise like nothing I'd ever heard before. I plugged my fingers in my ears until it stopped, and when it was quiet I made myself wait a little longer. Then I went outside.

The dog's tongue was hanging out like a soaked rag and there was blood on his teeth. I lifted him up, stiff already, and lowered him gently into the wheelbarrow. I took him down to the bottom of the garden and tipped up the barrow in front of the sty. He rolled out, his paws waving over in the air, and I pushed him inside too, as far as he would go.

I SIT by the bonfire on the upturned pail, the white hen folded in my lap. *Soon*, I tell myself, *it'll all be mended; the man, the sow, the dog, the chickens and the mistakes we made of it all.* I'm hunched up, hiding myself in the pouring rain. In a moment I'll get up and carry on, but for now I let the tears come.

Soon I'm stiff and soaked right through, but the tears are slowing and they'll stop before too long. In the wet, the fire will die down quickly, safe to leave to burn itself out. All that'll be left is a few charred pieces, easy to scatter and rake away.

I wipe my nose on the sleeve of my mac and get up, cradling the last of the hens. I bring her down to the pigsty and crawl inside, nestling us both down amongst the dark shapes.

It's New Year's Eve and I've come to him at last. The house and garden are empty now. I've scrubbed out all the sadness and wrong-doings. Now we'll lie together, Jamie and me, like Noah and his wife with all the animals in the ark. I scoop the earth with the heels of my hands, making a hollow in the lee of his shoulder. The rain pummels the roof as I tuck myself in.

Here in the dark, I can make our home over, begin again the way it was always meant to be. The dog will leap and chase its tail in the yard and the sow will snuffle at the swill we've put out. Our marriage will be blessed with a child born healthy, and even the curtains we'll hang anew. And Jamie and I will hold each other, no flinching or raging in the warmth of our bed, while the shining moon looks in at the window, and the land lies still and the child sleeps sound, and the hens roost nightly in the silver birch.

PHILIPPA EAST GREW up in Scotland and studied psychology and philosophy at the University of Oxford before moving to London to train as a clinical psychologist. Her debut novel *Little White Lies* was shortlisted for the CWA John Creasey New Blood Dagger. She has since published two further psychological suspense novels, *Safe and Sound* and *I'll Never Tell*, and is currently working on her fourth. Philippa now lives in the Lincolnshire countryside with her spouse and cat, and alongside her writing she continues to work as a psychologist and therapist.

Twitter: @philippa_east

amazon.co.uk/Philippa-East/e/B07S3JQDGK

I SPENT MY TIME RUNNING

TIM EWINS

My left foot landed.

I'm so grateful I'm not gay. That really wouldn't have gone down well at school.

Everyone thought that I was a big mouth and that I talked too much, but I was actually very quiet. Every time I did say something I tried to make it funny, so it was noticed. It must have seemed like I was always talking. Sometimes people laughed and sometimes they didn't, and it was that uncertainty that made me nervous every time I spoke.

When I was fourteen, I told a group of boys that I liked watching the *Teletubbies*. They laughed. I used to like it when people laughed at the few things I said and so I told some more people that I liked the *Teletubbies*. People continued to laugh so I continued to tell people.

I got on well with girls, which made my dad proud of me, though I never understood why. When I was fifteen, I found out that none of the boys at school liked me. Liking the *Teletubbies* wasn't a good joke. People had laughed, but not with me.

My right foot landed.

I was much younger when I tried on my mum's make-up – maybe six or seven. I only did it once.

The lipstick broke and I stained the carpet with the mascara, which made my mum cross.

'Why did you want to put on Mummy's make up?' I remember being asked. It was odd because I'd never been asked why I did all the other naughty things I did. I was just told that I shouldn't do them.

'I want to be like Mummy.'

My left foot landed.

I understood my dad's pride at me having female friends when they started to grow breasts. He thought I'd made friends with them to play the long game – friends now and something else later.

I loved dinosaurs when I was younger. I still love dinosaurs. That's something from my childhood that never left me. There are lots of things that never left me. I still like trains, but I never play with them; I still like party rings, but no one ever offers them to me; and I still like women's clothes, but I don't wear them anymore.

My right foot landed.

I met Santa one year. Actually, I met him most years but one year stands out to me. The room had been decorated to look like Santa's grotto and there were baskets around the room, each with different unwrapped presents in them. After Santa had met us all and told us to be good this year, we were allowed to pick a present each.

There were cars or dinosaurs for the boys and floral stationery sets for the girls. I didn't make this distinction and I liked writing stories so I picked up a stationery set.

I'd made the wrong choice.

I do still watch films about dinosaurs, but I don't think it has anything to do with the floral stationery set. I just objectively think that they're awesome.

My left foot landed.

Eventually, I made a friend who was a boy. Most of his other friends were girls too.

I'd actually become slightly more popular as my secret study of what made people laugh had become more successful, so I held a party at my dad's house. At the end of the party my friend and I shared a bed because his house was a long way away. When my dad came home from his night shift he saw us both leave the same bedroom. He smiled at us, said hi and then went to bed. My friend left and I watched TV.

We still hung around with our girl friends too,

but it seemed more normal to be friends with another boy. It helped us to fit in more at school. All the other boys were friends with other boys.

When my dad woke up later that day, he asked if I was gay. He wanted me to know that it was OK if I was. I'm lucky to have my dad, but as I've said before, I'm not gay. That wouldn't have gone down well at school.

My right foot landed.

I never liked sport much because I'm not very competitive and it doesn't really have a plot. I didn't see the point of finding out if I liked watching sport or not by watching lots of different sports, but I did it anyway, because maybe, if I found a sport I liked, I would be more normal.

After a while I began to wish I could tell my dad I was gay. He really would have been fine with it and maybe then I would make more sense to him: my large collection of musical DVDs; the sheer enjoyment I got from dancing like Freddie Mercury; my clothes. People at school called me gay to insult me, so when my dad asked me if I was gay, it felt like an attack, but it wasn't.

Wrestling has a plot and I did quite enjoy the storylines between matches, but then I realised that

I could watch similar storylines in soaps without having to endure any fighting, so I started watching *Home and Away* instead.

My left foot landed.

As for *playing* sport …
•Football: too long.
•Rugby: too confusing.
•Cricket: I'm no good at catching.
•Basketball: ditto.
•Ice hockey: I don't want to get hurt (and if that wasn't a possibility, the person in goal shouldn't have to dress like they do).

The main thing that put me off all these sports though, was the prospect of letting the other boys down.

•Netball: I'm not a girl.
•Field hockey: I'm not a girl.

Girls don't get as many options in sport, do they? I'm sort of jealous of that.

Home and Away got pretty good in the early 2000s. When I told people that I liked it, some of them laughed, so I stopped telling people that I liked it. I'm not falling for that again.

My right foot landed.

My friend who was a boy pretended to like football. He didn't really like it though. He talked about it with other boys, but I was often with him when the games were actually on.

We watched one game at my dad's house. My friend talked about Coldplay all the way through it. When he talked about the match to other boys at school he didn't mention Coldplay once, nor did he mention that by the time the game had finished, we had started writing funny poetry together. I didn't mind though. I understood.

He said that he liked the Olympics too, but it wasn't on that year so I don't know if he was pretending.

My left foot landed.

The year before I went to university I started running. With each step I found myself further away from people.

My right foot landed.

Who am I? Am I who I am supposed to be?

My left foot landed.

Am I a real man? And, if not, is my dad still proud of me?

I think so, yes; he is. But what about everybody else? I don't fit in. Are girls' clothes on boys funny, or do I just like them? Does that even matter? I think it does.

My right foot landed.

It does matter. It clearly does matter. Maybe I shouldn't have said that thing I said three weeks ago. It was a bit camp. I hope I fall in love one day. Girls don't fall in love with boys like me though, do they? I wish I was gay.

Girls fall in love with men and I'm not a real man. I'll probably die alone.

These are the things I used to think when I was running. That's why I spent my time running.

My left foot landed and I was miles away from everyone.

When I left school, I met a girl and I used to wear her coat. I liked the way it pulled my body in at the waist, making my shoulders look bigger. She liked that too. I also liked the fluffy hood and the diamanté around the stitching on the pockets.

I began to run less often.

My right foot landed.

Eventually, people caught up with me and I was no longer alone. My friends who are girls. My friend who is a boy. My dad. They all caught up. The girl I met after I left school made me understand that it was OK for me to be who I was and who I still am. I don't know her now. I know me.

My left foot landed. My right foot landed and I stopped.

TIM EWINS HAS PREVIOUSLY WRITTEN for DNA Mumbai, had two short stories highly commended and published in Michael Terence Short Story Anthologies, and had a very brief acting stint (he's in the film Bronson, somewhere in the background). *We Are Animals* is his first novel, with his second, *The Tiny Pieces of Enid*, coming soon.

Twitter: @EwinsTim
Instagram: @tim_ewins_author
eye-books.com/books/we-are-animals

THE OLD RAILWAY

POLLY CROSBY

As he waited on the platform for the five-fifteen to take him home from work, the young man noticed her again. In the last few months, as more and more men had enlisted, the station had grown quieter, and it was easy to spot her now.

She was always there, always a little further down the platform. She seemed so caught up in her own world, watching the goings-on around her curiously, as if she wasn't a part of it, as if she was only a spectator in this world.

He watched as she pulled an apple out of her bag. For a moment it gleamed in the sun, and then her fingers slipped on the waxy skin and it fell to the ground, rolling along the platform. It came to rest at his feet, and he bent down and picked it up. Already, bruises were blooming on the bright green skin.

Heart in his mouth, he strolled over to her and handed it back, trying to think of something witty to say but only managing to mumble, 'Here.'

'Thank you,' she said, offering him a small smile, the first he had seen from her, and it gave him courage.

'I have a spare apple, saved from lunch.' He opened his briefcase and rummaged around, pulling out papers and pens and spectacles, and then, at last, a small, red fruit. 'You're welcome to it.'

The shy smile was still there, little dimples of pink on her cheeks now. 'Oh, I couldn't.'

'It's no bother. Look, why don't we share it?' He held his breath at the presumption.

'All right,' she said. In the distance, they could hear the chug of the train approaching.

They managed to find two seats next to each other, and as the train pulled out of the station he blushed as she swayed against him. He took a little silver knife from his briefcase and began to slice the apple, offering her pieces of the sweet, white fruit. They sat and ate, licking their lips and smiling at one another.

All too soon, the train began to slow. 'This is my stop,' she said, getting to her feet.

His heart plummeted. The journey was too short. Tomorrow, he knew, they would go back to being strangers.

'Same time tomorrow?' she asked, and he grinned.

The apple became a daily ritual, the journey back from work the highlight of their day. In their little part of Suffolk, it hardly felt as if there was a war on at all.

A few months later, they were sitting in their

usual carriage, sharing the view of fields and trees as the countryside beyond whizzed past in a blur. It was quiet in the carriage – only one other person, an old man reading a newspaper at the other end – and they huddled close to one another, cherishing the rhythm of the train that pushed them together.

The little knife winked in the sunshine as he sliced into the day's apple, parting the pips from the flesh. As always, he offered her the first slice, and then he lifted the pips to the sunlight to see them better. They were brown and fat and shiny, bursting with life, and he took them between finger and thumb, and brought them to his lips for a kiss.

She laughed, then. 'What are you doing?'

'For luck,' he said simply. Pulling down the window, he launched them outside, watching them scatter among the trees. 'We'll have a picnic out there one day.' He nodded at the woodland on the edge of the village as the train lurched forward. 'Perhaps there'll be a little apple sapling there, blossoming just for us.'

She turned and followed his gaze as the landscape began to move swiftly in a blur, imagining the little pips burrowing deep into the soil, sending up shoots that would one day be trees so tall they would tower over her head.

'We can come back each year,' he said. 'Late

August, just as the apples are rosying up, and we can lie under its branches, marvelling at how it's grown.' There was a tinge of melancholy to his words.

'I'd like that,' she said, but she suddenly felt a great sweep of sadness.

'I need to tell—'

'You've been called up,' she interrupted him.

He nodded. The apple she had been eating tasted all of a sudden sour, and she placed the uneaten half in her lap.

'Will you wait?' he said, shifting in his seat to look at her, his hand at her chin, tilting her face so he could see into her eyes.

'Of course I'll wait, you daft thing,' she said, nudging him, and he pressed his lips to hers.

———

As MORE AND more men were called up, as the train became less and less crowded, she often found she had a whole carriage to herself. It seemed so silent without him, the seat no longer creaking as he sat down next to her, the smell of cut apple no longer a part of her journey.

She followed the news as best she could, and she wrote to him, even though she was never sure exactly where he was. Occasionally a letter came back, telling her he was just fine.

And then the letters stopped.

On the day she received a letter from his mother she was out in the garden, picking apples from the little Bramley tree for a pie. As she opened the envelope, the smell of the apples on her fingers drifted up to her nose, making her dizzy, and she knew, before reading it, what it said.

As SHE GREW OLDER, after the railway line was closed down, after she married and had children of her own, she sometimes took a bus ride on her own along the road that ran parallel with the old railway line, remembering.

It was a beautiful stretch, the water meadows flooded with soft spring rain, bringing clouds of water birds. If she caught it at the exact right moment, the pools of water would shine with the gold of the setting sun. The trees that grew, wild and unkempt, along the old disused railway track were always in silhouette, and she sometimes imagined an apple tree growing there, twisting up through the tangle of woodland across the years.

ONE HUNDRED YEARS since the young man fell, the creak of a gate in a meadow set geese flying into the air. A group of people came, carrying shovels and secateurs over their shoulders. The men and women searched the ground for the old railway track, lost to time. With careful hands, they began to clear the iron rails of decades of wildness, moving slowly out into the breathtaking beauty of the landscape. The trees here were overgrown, their black branches twisting and clasping together, bramble cables and hawthorns pricking and stabbing at the hardworking hands.

The group stopped for a rest on the edge of the track, passing around flasks of tea and flapjacks. The sun broke overhead, and one of them turned to look into the tangle of trees.

'What's that?' he said, getting to his feet and pointing to something, deep in the woodland. It appeared to glow, a cool, white light, beckoning them in.

They abandoned their picnic and began to cut at the brambles, clambering through the twining trees, getting closer and closer to the light.

'Well, I never,' a woman said. 'How did it survive out here?'

In a little glade, covered in trembling white blossom, an old apple tree stood, its boughs weighed down by a froth of flowers.

The group stood, looking at the tree, breathing in the scent of the blossom, and for a brief moment, each one of them could taste apples.

POLLY CROSBY GREW up on the Suffolk coast, and now lives with her husband and son in the heart of Norfolk. Polly was awarded both the Annabel Abbs Creative Writing Scholarship and the Felicia Yapp Scholarship for her debut novel, *The Illustrated Child*, which came runner up in The Bridport Prize. She is currently working on her third novel, *Vita and the Birds*, out in 2023.

pollycrosby.com
Twitter: @writerpolly
Instagram: @writerpolly

THE DEBATE

PENNY BATCHELOR

The traffic queue on the motorway stretched snake-like, slithering across the countryside as far as the eye could see; cars, lorries and vans stopping and starting in a randomly choreographed dance with no determinable end.

Above the carriageway a sign flashed: *30mph. Accident ahead.*

'Accident, yeah right,' she said, flicking her eyes towards him in the driver's seat, back and forth in quick motion. A deep breath in, then out came the question she'd stored up to ask. 'What if you had to choose between shooting me dead or killing a random person you didn't know? Who would you choose?'

Her fingers tapped rhythmically on the passenger seat dashboard in a way that never ceased to grate him. Quickly, his foot alternated between short pumps on the accelerator followed by sharp stamps on the brake.

He jerked his head towards her, only half listening. 'Hmm … I'd take the gun off him so he couldn't shoot anyone.'

Light rain fell on the car, triggering the windscreen wipers to turn on automatically. Checking his rear-view mirror, he reasoned that the 4x4 behind him was driving too close and decided to stop dead until a decent gap opened up in front.

'Who says it's a man? It could be a woman. And anyway, you only have one choice – shoot me or someone else.'

Was it a bead of sweat she saw appear on his forehead? The resulting silence amplified the tap-tap of her nails, acrylic against plastic.

Only when their car was stationary did he turn his attention to the question. 'Well then I'd choose to save you of course.' He sighed. 'Are we going there again?' Glancing at the dashboard clock he saw that it wasn't long until the hourly news bulletin on Radio 4. He'd switch the radio on a minute before to be sure not to miss the beginning.

Yes, it is *a bead of sweat*, she thought, as it dropped down his cheek and he swiped it away with the back of his hand. She twisted her torso to face him, pushing her chestnut hair behind her left ear as she usually did when she was thinking about something. He used to find it endearing.

Used to.

He instinctively flinched when he caught a glimpse of what her hair had covered.

'Yes we are going there again,' she replied. 'So it's OK for someone else to die? Some other family to lose their loved one?'

'No of course it's not OK, but you asked me to choose and I picked you.'

'What if it was a little toddler that got shot?'

'I wouldn't know, would I? You said it would be someone random.' *Not now*, he thought. *Not again.*

The windscreen wipers changed to extra-fast mode as the rain fell more heavily. Darkness descended, with grey clouds shrouding the sun. He turned on the car's headlights. Someone to the front of them impatiently beeped their horn. He rolled his eyes. 'What's the point of doing that? It's not going to magically clear the road.'

A car's jarring beep, coming from the other side of the carriageway when a lorry pulled out right in front of it, broke the minute's silence that followed.

'What if you had to choose between me or ten random people being shot?' she asked.

'I'd still choose you. Is this a test? Are you trying to ask me how much I love you?'

The diamond set into her wedding ring twinkled as she twisted the band around her finger. 'No, it's not a test, I'm interested to know. That's ten people who would die. That's a lot of death just to save me.'

'Well of course I'd want to save you, you're my wife. It's only human nature to want to save those you love. I wouldn't know the other ten people. I'd be sad, yes, that they were shot, but I'd rather them than you,' he clipped.

The car's clock marked the passing of another unit of time.

'So you wouldn't feel guilty, then, that those ten people's deaths would be on your hands? Ten frightened people with families who'd be distraught?'

'But they wouldn't be my responsibility, would they? You said the only choice I had was to choose you or ten random strangers to die. It wouldn't be me who shot them, it would be the murderer's fault.' Try as he might, he didn't manage to mask the irritation and confusion breaking into his voice.

Air. She needed more air. She opened the window a little but shut it again when rain spat onto her face. 'What about a hundred people?'

'Can we not do this now? We're going to be late getting to your sister's.' The cars in front of him ploughed ahead and the pointer on his speedometer inched further to the right.

'I said, what about a hundred people?'

The 4x4 behind inched even closer. 'Oh, I don't know … I'd tell the murderer to find a hundred people who were on their deathbeds and shoot them.'

'You can't. It's random strangers who get shot, not hospice patients.

'Can't hospice patients be part of a random sample of people?'

'You're not getting the point here.' She turned her head towards the passenger window. He exhaled and jabbed the button to switch on the radio, prompting her to turn around to him, punching her forefinger on the radio's off button and saying, 'Not the news again, God knows I was on it enough. Why do you never, ever get the point?'

He slapped the steering wheel in exasperation. 'What do you want me to say? That I'm sorry, again, for the umpteenth time? Just tell me. That I'd have a million people shot to save you? Do you want me to shoot myself? Or choose to have you shot? Is that it? Do you want me to be the monster here?'

'Well, you didn't save me before, did you?'

He noticed at the last possible second that the car in front had come to halt and managed to stop just a centimetre behind it. The 4x4 behind their hatchback did an emergency stop and sounded its horn ferociously. He was about to flick the v sign when he thought twice. Now was not the time for a road rage encounter. He didn't want to be that man.

A few seconds passed in silence. He struggled to

answer in a calm, reasonable tone, the one she'd never told him she hated. 'You know how bad I feel about that. How many times do I have to tell you? I was drunk. I didn't pick up your messages. I am so, so sorry. Every day I wish I could turn back the clock, but I can't. What more can I do?'

Although in the morning she had gone about her daily routine of putting thick foundation on her face, when his eyes caught hers the soft pink scar that smiled from the corner of her nose to her ear seemed brighter, as if it were taunting his masculine inadequacy.

'*Sorry, sorry* – it's just a word. You weren't there when I needed you. The worst point of my life and you weren't there for me. I was all on my own. I couldn't fight. I needed you to do that and you didn't come.'

'What's brought this on again? I thought we were OK, that you were over it?'

'Over it? That'd suit you, wouldn't it? Pretend it never happened, that everything's fine. Do you honestly think I'll ever get over it? You have no idea how frightened I was.'

'No, of course I didn't mean you were over what happened, but I thought you'd stopped being angry with me. We talked, didn't we? Discussed it? Had counselling?' Traffic just started to move again when a car in the outside lane swerved into the small gap he had left in front. 'Prick!'

'I lied. I said I was OK to shut you up. You turned everything around until it was all about you. Not about me being attacked, but your guilt.' Everything she'd kept inside came up with bile.

'I didn't know you felt that way.'

'Well I'm telling you now.' She plucked a thin, black hairband from around her wrist and fiercely tied her hair up in a messy ponytail. No more hiding.

'So, tell me,' she went on, gathering momentum, 'what is the point to my question? If you had the choice of someone either shooting me or a random person you don't know, which would you choose?'

'I don't know; honestly, I don't know. Are you going to leave me?' For a second his voice wavered like a nervous little boy's.

'Think! What is the point?' She was shouting now, their enclosed box insulating them from the outside world, the sleety, black rain obscuring them from the view of other drivers. The car carried on moving but his concentration was firmly off the road.

'Just tell me! How am I supposed to know if you don't tell me? I'm not a mind reader!'

'You're supposed to be prepared to die with me!' she screamed. 'If you can't save me then go with me – by my side, all the way. "Till death us do part" you promised in front of witnesses until once again you put your sodding work mates and the pub before me!'

'I didn't know you'd being calling me! I didn't know she'd followed you home. I was stupid and pissed and I'm sorry.' That word again. He started to sob. The tears in his eyes blurred his vision. The orange halo of the lights merged into an ominous glow.

'I told you, sorry is not good enough. It was your ex-girlfriend! If you'd been there you might have been able to talk her down or physically stop her!'

The 4x4 behind beeped its horn again and instinctively he slammed his foot on the accelerator to get away, to create as much distance from it as he could. In the split second it took for him to blink the tears from his eyes, he realised that he wouldn't be able to stop in time to avoid hitting the car in front. Swerving left into a gap on the inside lane, his car skidded and clipped the car in front. The 4x4 sped past, but a lorry behind crashed straight into the back of the hatchback at an angle, sending it head-on into the arms of the unforgiving crash barrier.

Brakes screeched and a few people sounded their horns in warning, but inside the car all that could be heard was the sports news: Manchester United had lost 2:1 to Chelsea. Her hand had hit the on button as her body lurched towards the dashboard.

'Next on Radio 4 – *The Archers*.' The jaunty theme tune was the last thing they ever heard.

PENNY BATCHELOR is the author of two psychological thrillers published by RedDoor Press: *My Perfect Sister*, which was longlisted for The Guardian's Not The Booker Prize 2020 and was also a Waitrose Weekend pick, and *Her New Best Friend*, described by Lovereading.co.uk as 'a white-knuckle tense thriller that has more twists than a Simone Biles gymnastics routine.' She is the co-founder of the #KeepFestivalsHybrid campaign and the Authors With Disabilities and Chronic Illnesses Literary Prize, launched in 2022. Penny lives in Warwickshire with her husband.

pennybatchelor.co.uk

Twitter: @penny_author

Instagram: @pennybatchelorauthor

Facebook: @pennyauthor

THE LASKOWSKI BROTHERS

DEBRA BARNES

Metz, 1937

'Tell us a story, Maman,' pleaded my younger brother, Samuel. Little Claude was already half asleep, tucked up in bed. Papa was not yet home from work, which wasn't unusual; this time he had gone to Paris to choose some new fabrics and was expected back late that night.

'Which story would you like today?' asked Maman.

'The one when you meet Papa!' I said.

'No! Tell us a story about dragons and knights!' said Samuel.

Maman laughed kindly. 'How about I get a book with stories of dragons and knights to read to you another time? Tonight, I'll tell you about life in Poland and tomorrow night I'll tell you about how I met your father.'

'All right,' agreed Samuel, reluctantly.

'Get under the covers first,' said Maman, busying herself with our blankets. 'My parents, Bubbe and Zayde, grew up in a small Polish village. On one side lived the Jewish families like theirs, and on the other side lived the Cossacks. The Jews and

93

the Cossacks didn't bother each other, usually. Everyone lived in small houses, not like the apartment blocks we have here. Many families kept some animals and grew their own vegetables. Most of the Jewish families in the village were very religious. The boys studied the Talmud and prayed while the girls helped their mothers look after younger brothers and sisters, learnt to be good Jewish wives and how to keep a kosher home. The only way for a boy to meet a girl was to be introduced through a relative, or maybe a Rabbi or a matchmaker. Although they had grown up in the same village, Bubbe and Zayde had not met until they were introduced by the matchmaker. They were married a few weeks later. They didn't get much say in the matter but as we all know they went on to have a long and contented life together.'

Samuel couldn't stop himself. 'But Bubbe is always miserable!'

'Shhh now, that is unkind. She has many ailments these days that make life difficult, but it wasn't always that way. Once, they were young and happy. They left the village soon after they married to make their home in a town called Białystok. That's where I was born at the beginning of the new century. I was the youngest of many brothers and sisters; as you know, Uncle Isaac is much older than me. Zayde began to make clothes, both Shabbat-best and work clothes to wear in the coal mines. He built up quite a business, but bad things were happening to the Jewish people.'

'What sort of bad things?' I asked.

'Nothing for you to worry about, my darlings,' said Maman, smoothing down my hair. 'We're far away from all that now and nothing like that would ever happen in France.'

I wasn't so sure Maman was right. Did she not know about the Jew-hating kids at school? I decided to keep my doubts to myself and she continued with the story.

'Many Jews left Poland to live in other countries, like my sister Cloe who went to England. Some went to America—'

'I wish we could go to America,' I said, unable to stop myself from interrupting once more.

'Maybe you will one day. A lot of people were also coming to France which was welcoming immigrants—'

'Like Charlie Chaplin!' exclaimed Samuel. Maman and Papa had taken Samuel and I to the movie theatre to watch *The Immigrant*. We all loved the funny little man with the sad face and strange way of walking who travelled to America on a big boat.

'Well, yes, like Charlie Chaplin in his moving picture. You see, millions of French people had died during the war, and the French politicians wanted more people to come and live here but actually, when we left Poland in 1919, Bubbe and Zayde were intending to take us all to America.'

'Was Papa with you?'

'No, we didn't meet till later. It was me with Bubbe and Zayde, Uncle Isaac and Aunt Alisa. We came to France by train; it took days and we had to travel through Czechoslovakia, Austria and Germany to get here. The plan was to go to Le Havre. Do you know where that is?' I shook my head. 'It's a port on the opposite side of France to where we live, on the west coast. That was where we would catch a boat for America.'

'Why didn't you go?'

'When we got here to Metz it was only supposed to be a stopover, but as we arrived on the train Zayde saw the coal mines, like the ones back in our town in Poland, and he thought it was a sign from God. Zayde said' – and here Maman put on his thick Polish accent – '"What would I do in New York or London anyway, in a big city like one of those? If we stay here in Metz, I can build up another clothing business just like the one I was forced to abandon in Poland. *B'ezrat Hashem*, with

God's help.'" We all giggled at her impression. 'Zayde could make work clothes for the miners and factory workers and smart clothes for the growing Jewish community to wear on Shabbat. And so, we settled in Metz.

'During our first years here, many Jews continued to flee Poland and stop in Metz to catch a train to the coast where they could board a ship for America. Every Friday Zayde would go to the railway station to pick up any Orthodox Jews who didn't want to continue their journey over the Sabbath. He would bring them home and we would feed them, give them somewhere to sleep, and Zayde would take them to synagogue with him. Everyone in Metz agreed that this was a great act of kindness, although Bubbe sometimes wished that he would take a week off from being such a mensch and maybe we could have a Shabbat when he didn't bring waifs and strays home with him. I remember there being strangers staying with us almost every week; it drove Bubbe to her wits' end. We didn't have a big home, so depending on how many there were on a particular night, the travelling visitors would often have to bed down on the furniture or the floor, covered with blankets and tablecloths. If there were any young girls staying, I would share my bed with them. I didn't really mind, I was happy to help, and now … it's time for you to go to bed too!'

'Aww, more please Maman,' said Samuel.

'More tomorrow. Now go to sleep. Goodnight, my darling boys.'

As I lay in bed that night, I wondered what it would have been like if Maman had been older and gone to England like Aunt Cloe instead of staying in France. I was used to being called a 'dirty Jew' by boys in the street, but that didn't make it easier to live with and I worried for my younger brothers. Hitler had come to power when I was in kindergarten and there were many Germans living in Metz who were followers of *der Führer*, as they called him. When I asked Maman if she ever wished that she had been older and gone to live in England with Aunt Cloe she said that if she hadn't come to France then she wouldn't have met Papa and then I wouldn't have been born. On the really bad days, that didn't seem to be such a terrible alternative.

SAMUEL

Claude covered his face with his hands and peered gingerly through his little fingers at the photograph. Our grandmother stared into the distance with a look of boredom while our grandfather seemed terrifying with the huge scar on his forehead. Papa said the scar had been left by a Cossack trying to cut his head off. Not only had the attack failed, but Papa said our grandfather had then cut the Cossack's head off in retaliation.

'If you don't do what I tell you, the ghost of Grandfather will come and haunt you in your sleep!' I said, shaking the photograph frame menacingly in front of Claude's face.

'No, please!' Claude begged.

'Will you do my chores for me tomorrow?'

'Yes, anything!'

'Fine,' I said, taking one more look at our grandfather before returning the frame to its rightful place on our parents' bedroom wall. He certainly had the look of someone you wouldn't mess with, and Papa had inherited his strong build. Sadly, it hadn't been passed down to me which is why I needed props when I wanted to torment my little brother. He was also my best buddy, but I couldn't resist getting the upper hand. It wasn't in my nature to be cruel, but that afternoon I'd been chased home from school yet again by the bully Jew-haters and I needed to let off steam. Claude was the only one who allowed me to boss him about. Most likely he was only pretending to be scared to please me. That's the kind of sweet kid he was.

'Let's play Cossacks and Jews!' Claude shouted as he ran to the kitchen and grabbed a large wooden spoon to wield as a sword. 'I'll be the Cossack!'

'And I'll be Grandfather!' I replied, grabbing the wooden rolling pin from under the hands of Bubbe who was just about to roll out some pastry for *rugelach*, those delicious, sweet cakes she liked to make.

'Who took the rolling pin?' Bubbe demanded. 'Bring it back right now!'

'No one,' I replied. 'You must have put it down somewhere.'

'Don't be cheeky with me, young man. I may be blind, but I have a good idea who it was. Just wait until I tell your poor dear mother. And no *rugelach* for either of you boys tonight unless it is returned to me RIGHT NOW!'

'Here it is, Bubbe,' I said sweetly, placing the rolling pin in her hands. 'It was on the table next to you all the time. Hmm, that *rugelach* looks delicious. I'm guessing I will get a double portion for being the one to find your rolling pin?'

'Get out of the kitchen before I hit you on the head with it,' said Bubbe.

'You'd have to find me first!' I taunted, as Claude and I ran out laughing.

PIERRE

Samuel and Claude were sitting on the floor, their noses stuck in a comic book. Samuel was reading out loud while pointing with his finger so our little brother could follow along by looking at the pictures. I was engrossed in the new issue of *Le Miroir des Sports* that Papa had brought back from Paris. Football was my passion and there was a report on the match the week before when France had battered Belgium to a 3-1 defeat.

When Maman came into the room, Samuel and I put our comics and magazines away and got into bed; we didn't want to waste a moment of her precious time and were all eager for her to fulfil her promise by telling us the story of how she and Papa met.

'I was sent to the home of a family and introduced to a young man,' she began. 'We were left alone in the dining room while his parents went into the kitchen. I sat upright at the dining table, my hands in my lap. My gaze was fixed on the linen tablecloth. I remember it was very beautiful and I admired the tidy stitchwork and intricate pattern.

The young man sitting opposite me cleared his throat, causing me to look up at him. "Your family came from Białystok?" he asked. "Yes," I told him. "I was nineteen years old when we came to France."

'I should have asked where in Poland he was from and when he came to France, but I had no interest in making the meeting any longer than it had to be. "I really must be going now. I have errands to run for my mother," I said after a short while, hoping that I was not being rude. "Of course, of course. May God bless and protect your beloved mother," said the young man. "Well, goodbye," I said as I stood up. I hurried out of the apartment building and ran home.

'When Bubbe heard the front door open she called out, "Clara, is that you?" I replied that it was. "So? How did it go? Was he nice?" she asked me. "Very nice, I'm sure. But not for me," I said. "Ach, not again! What was the matter with this one?" she said. "He was so boring, Mame. He had nothing interesting to say and no sense of humour. He was so pale and skinny. And he was so shy, like a little mouse," I told her.

'Zayde came in to join us. "It sounds like you could have eaten him for breakfast!" he joked. "Shush now!" said Bubbe. "This is the third suitor the matchmaker has introduced to her, and she always says the same."

'I told her, "Because all three have been the same: shy, religious and dull! That's not the type of man I want to marry. I know that's how you and Papa met, but we live in a different country now and life is not the same. I want to marry for love."

'Bubbe looked upset. She said, "Your father and I love each other very much." I should have chosen my words with more care. "I know. I didn't mean that you don't love each other. But you were lucky. You didn't choose each other, you were introduced. You married first and after you learnt to love. It could have been very different."

'She said, "That is true. Look at poor Mrs Weinblatt from the synagogue; what a scoundrel her husband is! And Mrs Baum from the market; her husband is a tyrant – he won't even let her buy new shoes when the soles of hers are full of holes. But Clara darling, you are twenty-one years old now. I had three children already by the time I was your age."

'I told her, "Mame! Twenty-one is not old these days." Bubbe threw her hands up in defeat. "Yes, yes. I know. Things are different now!"

'I said, "Don't worry, Mame. I do want to get married, but only when I meet the right man for me. I need to get changed now. I'm going to dinner with the Shapiros this evening."

"'So, maybe Mr Right will be there tonight?" quipped Zayde. "*Baruch Hashem*, please God," said Mame.'

'I CHOSE MY CLOTHES CAREFULLY,' my mother continued. 'I knew my parents had only been joking about me meeting my future husband that evening, but Mimi Shapiro had told me about an acquaintance of her husband who was also invited for dinner. Most of my friends were married now, and I had no wish to be single and living with my parents forever. Mimi knew me well and she said that I would like him. I took off the long sleeved, high neck dress I was wearing and changed into something more modern, with a pretty pattern.'

'Like the dresses Papa sells?' I asked.

'Yes, exactly like the dresses Papa sells,' replied Maman, with a smile. 'Then I put on the new lipstick I had bought from Paris; I wanted to make sure I looked nice.'

'You always look beautiful, Maman,' said Samuel.

'Thank you, darling. When I arrived at her

apartment, Mimi introduced us. "Clara Hofman, this is Jankiel Laskowski," she said.'

'Who's Jankiel?' asked Samuel.

'That's Papa's real name, silly,' I told my brother.

'Why does Papa have two names?' asked Claude, who was getting very confused.

'Because he is a spy, like the man in the comic!' declared Samuel excitedly.

'Papa is a spy?' said Claude.

'No, my darling,' said Maman. 'Papa is just Papa.'

'Carry on, Maman,' I said.

'Jankiel offered me his hand and said, "Call me Albert, please. I don't use Jankiel anymore." His handshake was firm but gentle although his hands were rough – he was working as a stone mason back then. I asked if he was from Poland like myself. It was obvious that he was Polish, but I wanted to keep talking to him. He said he was from Lodz and had come to France about four years earlier. I told him I came with my family around that time too. He said he had come alone.

'He asked how I spent my time. I told him, "I'm the youngest daughter and the only one still living with my parents, so I help. Mainly I run errands, but I also assist with the family business.

My father has a clothing company and contracts work out all over the town; many people work for him cutting, sewing and finishing garments." Then he asked me what I like to do for myself. I said I like taking walks in the park, reading books on many different subjects and meeting new people when I come to my friends for dinner! He smiled when I said that. Later Papa said when he saw me, he fell instantly in love with my beautiful almond-shaped eyes.'

'Did you fall instantly in love with him?' I asked, thankful that none of my friends could hear me talking about something so girly and romantic.

'Not exactly,' replied Maman, laughing. 'He was clean and tidy, which was a good start. He looked very strong – he was a champion amateur wrestler in those days, and he was polite. I thought he was nice but I knew that my parents wouldn't approve of him because I could see he was not religious, so we just chatted about nothing in particular and I didn't think I would see him again after that evening.'

'But you did!'

'Yes, I did. A few days later I went for a walk and who should I bump into on the street corner right outside my home, but your father! I thought it was just coincidence, although I was pleased to see him because I'd thought about him a few times since we met. He later confessed to pestering our friends to tell him where my family lived, and he'd waited hours for me to appear that afternoon so that we could "accidentally" run into each other.'

'I can't believe Papa did that,' I said.

'Maybe one day you will meet a girl who will make you want to do silly things too,' said Maman. 'After our first "chance" meeting Papa would often wait for me in the street outside my home and walk with me to the library or to the park, or accompany me on my errands. I grew very fond of this strong and determined young man who was courting me.'

'But what about Papa?' said Samuel.

'I'm talking about Papa, silly! We would go for walks in the riverside parks on Sabbath afternoon, chatting about the difficult lives we'd left behind in Poland and about how life was also challenging here in France, but in different ways. I told him about the letters I received from my sister Cloe in London, and Alisa who had only just gone to live in New York. I reminded Papa that my parents would not approve of him, but he just smiled and nodded. After a couple of months, we met one day on the corner of my street, as usual, and walked to the botanical gardens. It was further than the other parks, but Papa insisted. He seemed nervous that afternoon. It was early spring 1924, and the magnificent magnolia tree was in bloom. After checking around us and when he was sure that no one was watching, Papa picked a blossom from the tree and placed it in my hair. He took my hands in his and asked me to be his wife.'

It was no secret that there had been objections. After he proposed to Maman, Papa went to ask Zayde for permission to marry. My grandfather could see that this young suitor was not the religious man they had hoped for their youngest daughter. It was, however, clear that he was honest and hardworking and smitten. Maybe, Zayde and Bubbe reasoned later between themselves, their daughter would be better off with a strong wrestler rather than a feeble scholar, the way the world was going. These days Jewish people needed to be able to protect themselves and their families as much as they needed to pray and study the Torah, and besides, they told each other, this marriage would be preferable to having their Clara left on the shelf. Time was running out ('twenty-one already!') and here was the first man she had not rejected.

'Then you married Papa and lived happily ever after,' said Claude.

'No,' said Samuel. 'First they had three sons. The eldest son was a bit boring' – that's when I punched Samuel on the arm – 'the middle son was fantastic' – we all groaned – 'and the third son was too tiny to make a difference. And *then* they lived happily ever after!'

Maman laughed. 'Thank you, Samuel,' she said, 'although maybe the story is not finished quite yet.' And with that Maman put her hand to her stomach, and with a knowing smile kissed us all goodnight.

***

DEBRA BARNES is the author of *The Young Survivors*, a novel based on her mother's incredible story of survival during the Holocaust. Debra is committed to educating and informing others about the dangers of racism and hatred. She tells her mother's story in schools for the charity, Generation 2 Generation and works as Next Generations Manager for The Association of Jewish Refugees.

linktr.ee/DebraBarnes

Twitter: @debra_author

SHOW TIME

ANNA JEFFERSON

C laudia tightly grips the steering wheel of the brand new white Landcruiser with her manicured fingers and pushes the automatic up to fifty along the high street, propelled forward by adrenaline. She turns up Destiny's Child's *Survivor* to volume twelve and lowers the driver's window an inch. The bracing November wind whips through the crack, making her eyes water.

She slams on her brakes at a zebra crossing on North Road as a slow trickle of mid-morning shoppers drift across. A young man in a cheap suit walks purposefully, protecting his head from the rain with a free newspaper. An old woman hunches as she tugs a tartan trolly behind her; she turns her crumpled face to Claudia and shakes her head disapprovingly at the music. A gaggle of girls in the local comprehensive school uniform skip across, drinking cans of full-fat Coke and munching packets of crisps with a carelessness only afforded to the young with high metabolisms. A mother pushes a buggy, her face lined with fatigue and fear, as her eyes dart from the baby to the road to the baby again.

Claudia instinctively places her hand on her stomach, imagining the tiny foetus growing inside her – the size of a blueberry, according to the parenting websites. She revs the accelerator and tears through the town until the shops turn to terraced houses, then give way to the industrial estates and finally, the wide-open countryside.

She turns the windscreen wipers on full and opens both windows wide. The rain pelts through, stinging her face like a thousand tiny darts. Her silk shirt damply clings to her driving arm, but Claudia doesn't care. She just wants to feel something. Anything. Other than this gnawing, bitter resentment that eats her up inside like acid erosion. She pushes the car on, steering it at speed around the windy roads.

She sees the familiar sign. *Welcome to Calding. Please Drive Carefully Through Our Village.* It's the only indication she is driving through a village at all, a meagre row of terraced houses flanked by a Spar shop on one side and a garage on the other.

The ominous black clouds filter out any sunshine, and lights are on in all the houses, even though it's only eleven-thirty. She slows to a crawl and looks in one house and then the next. They look warm. Cosy. Net curtains, knick-knacks, photo frames and vases of dried flowers line the windowsills. She imagines how content the occupants must be. Leading their happy little lives with their happy little families.

She drives out of Calding and speeds up as the

narrow road takes a sharp turn, joining the dual carriageway. A juggernaut hurtles towards her, flashing its lights, horn beeping as she careers in front of it, inches to spare as she cuts it off; she thanks him briefly with a raised arm out of the open window.

The music is interrupted by a call coming through the speakers. She closes the windows and grips the wheel.

'Incoming call from My Man. Incoming call from My Man,' the stereo taunts. Her finger hesitates over the green phone symbol, before pressing *end call.* An icy shiver shudders down her spine and she turns on the heating full blast.

'Incoming call from My Man. Incoming call from My Man,' the stereo repeats.

This time, she presses *answer.*

'Claude? Where are you?' He asks loudly over the bustle of a coffee shop.

She stares ahead as the windscreen wipers cut through the pelting rain.

'Claudia? Can you hear me? I'm in Starbucks and it's fucking chaos in here. Everyone's chosen to come for lunch at the same time. Can I have the grilled cheese sandwich and a mocha, soya milk with a drop of caramel. Just a drop, mind – last time it tasted way too sweet. Just a splash, got it? Thanks. Claudia? Can you hear me?'

She drives on, gripping the wheel so tightly her wrists ache.

'Look, it's fucking mayhem in here. I don't know if you can hear me, but just wanted to let you know, I'm going to be late tonight. Don't worry about making anything for me, don't cook for me. I'll order something in. Fucking chaos. The right hand not speaking to the left, again. Anyway. Don't wait up, it's going to take an age to get through all the paperwork. I can't really hear you, to be honest, so I'll sign off. Love you. Is that mine? 'Scuse me, I think that's my order. Yep, mocha and a—' The line goes dead.

Claudia wonders how many conversations have taken place like that over the last two decades. Him speaking. Endlessly speaking at her. Droning on about work. About the gym. About what he's eaten or hasn't eaten. About a meeting he's been in. How great he was. How he owned the room. He's always owning rooms, whatever that means. How he made that deal. How he pumped the hand of this guy. How he was asked to play golf with that guy. How lucky they are. How very lucky they are to live the life they lead.

Fury starts to bubble in Claudia's gut. She feels

it rise in her throat like bile until she can contain it no longer and lets out a scream so loud her ears throb and her jaw aches. Tears stream down her cheeks.

She pats the passenger seat, locates her bottle of water and, after opening it with clenched thighs and one hand, gratefully gulps it down to extinguish the fire and daggers in the back of her mouth.

She needs a clear, calm voice to make the telephone calls.

Simon always had the unwavering confidence of someone who knew his worth, even if the world hadn't recognised it yet. Claudia wasn't long out of drama school when she'd first met him. He worked in IT but was adamant that he wasn't your clichéd computer geek.

'It's fast cash,' he told her, as he tried and failed to explain the rise of the internet to her.

'It won't take off,' she replied. 'It's a fad. What next? The whole world is going to be taken over by robots?' She laughed her infectious laugh.

'Well, let's see who's right,' he said knowingly and confidently, giving her a winning smile.

Their first flat together was above a chip shop.

Twice a day the front room filled up with the nauseating smell of the deep fat fryers. It clung to Claudia's clothes, to her hair. Other cast members commented on it in the green room. 'I feel hungry just standing next to you,' they would joke as they had a post-show beer after another half-filled auditorium had watched their modern-day rendition of *Much Ado About Nothing*.

'It's not always going to be like this,' Simon reassured her as she returned from the laundrette, having washed and tumble-dried every item of clothing she owned to pack for the outdoor market-town tour of *A Midsummer Night's Dream*. That evening they curled up on the sofa, dreamed up elaborate plans of what they would do when Simon's grand moneymaking schemes came to fruition, of the countries they would visit, the experiences they would have. Claudia loved Simon's hunger for life, however improbable it might be.

Two months later, a stone heavier from eating predominately takeaway food, and five hundred pounds down as the profit-shared show flopped at every venue, Claudia returned from the tour dispirited, to find Simon wired with excitement.

'Don't worry about the show,' he said with a flick of a wrist, trivialising her career as if she'd just forgotten something from the supermarket instead of spending the last two months living in filthy digs, sharing a room with two other actors, one who sleep talked, the other who sleep farted, and all she had to show for it was a rucksack full of clothes that no longer fitted her and an extended overdraft limit.

'I'm going to buy you a fucking theatre if you want one. Every day will be show time.' His pupils dilated, as if on drugs; he wrung his hands as he spoke, looping one around the other with nervous energy.

'What are you talking about?' Claudia asked as she shoved her clothes in the washing machine. Everything reeked of cigarettes.

'I told you things were going to take off, and they have. *We* have,' he nodded assuredly.

'Look Simon, I need a shower. I need to get some sleep in a half-decent bed. And then I need to get up early and start looking through the paper for a proper job,' she sighed.

Simon grabbed her by the arm and pulled her down to the sofa with him.

'Look,' he waved a piece of paper in front of her. 'Just look.'

She took it from him and unfolded a cheque made out to Simon Peterson for five thousand pounds.

Claudia's eyes darted from the cheque to Simon

to the cheque again, her mouth open in disbelief. 'What have you done? How did you get this?'

Simon paused for effect, cleared his throat dramatically and said, 'The internet, baby. I told you it would pay off. And this, this,' he snatched the cheque from her hand and waved it in the air, 'is just the beginning.'

Claudia didn't bother to shower. She climbed on top of Simon, they tugged each other's clothes off and fucked on the sofa with the heady aphrodisiac of success and imminent wealth.

Simon's investments carried huge risk and huge returns. He researched the dot.com businesses he supported, cashing in shares at the peak before the peak before the fall. While others were greedy, he was informed. Claudia and he made crude jokes about his ability to pull out at just the right moment. Which was ironic, as Claudia was becoming increasingly desperate to have a child.

Simon made his first million aged twenty-six. Claudia, of the same age, had swapped treading the boards for strutting next to Simon at high profile charity events.

Simon proposed to Claudia on her twenty-eighth birthday. They had been together for seven years. Their wedding felt like a public display of decadence, the reception taking place in the grounds of their mock-Tudor house. As she stood next to her new husband under a canopy of white roses, everyone cheered. But she caught eyes with her mum, who smiled weakly at her as she dabbed her eyes with a tissue.

Claudia suddenly felt desperately lost.

As Simon's wealth increased, the wedge between them grew. They laughed less. Bickered more. Talked without pleasantries.

'Where's my Paul Smith suit?'

'Try the wardrobe.'

'I have.'

'No, the one in the spare room.'

'I've tried that one too.'

'Well, what about the second guest room?'

'Why would it be in there?'

'I have no idea, Simon. Why don't you ask Susie? That's what you hire her for, isn't it?'

Claudia wondered what had happened to her. Where was the girl who wanted to be an actress?

The village they moved to reeked of new money and insecurity. Stockbrokers. Debt purchasers. Lottery winners. YouTube stars. Gamblers. Claudia's neighbours cast a wide vocational net. The women were fake, from their hair extensions to their nose jobs; from their impractically long nails to their year-round tans.

The men were charming and untrustworthy. They dined at each other's houses, drank at the same private clubs, bitched about each other relentlessly behind one another's backs. There was always something to do, but it was so vacuous. So pointless.

Not for the men, of course. They were in charge of the business. The women, however, had the important job of making themselves look forever young, or live with the consequences. Simon joked about them when they'd first seen the house.

'They look like they're from one of those awful programmes you watch,' he whispered behind a cupped hand when the estate agent showed them around. But as the weeks turned into months, he grew defensive of the people he'd been so happy to mock.

'You don't have to be such a bitch,' he snapped when she spoke about anyone from the village.

'Me. *Me?*' she replied, exasperated. 'These women are vile. They are literally awful to everyone. Sandra got the poor girl in the village shop sacked because she didn't know whether the toothpaste was vegan. It's fucking toothpaste. Who gives a shit if it's vegan or not? How can you defend them? Susie. Back me up here, will you?' Claudia tried to embroil Simon's PA into the conversation, but as always, she remained neutral and irritatingly professional.

'I haven't really spoken to them, Claudia,' she replied, eyes always on Simon to ensure that was the correct response.

So Claudia stopped caring. She went out with the women, she bitched with them, knowing they did the same about her when she wasn't there. She had her hair done. She got her tits fixed. She had her teeth whitened. She slowly started to phase out her old life and everyone in it. She reasoned with herself that it was a role. The ultimate role. The leading lady in her own life and she was playing it beautifully.

She even started to believe that this was the life she wanted. And why wouldn't she? She had everything she could ask for and more.

CLAUDIA PULLS UP on the roadside of the cul-de-sac. The rain has now eased off to a light sprinkling. Her huge car looks ridiculous next to the dirty grey Volvo estates and Kias. Claudia's eyes dart between the houses, trying to calculate how close she is to the driveways; she panics that she's blocking someone's vehicle, either in front of her or behind.

She turns the key in the ignition and fusses with moving forward a couple of inches, then backwards again, the parking sensor beeping wildly as she does. She can feel the sweat on the back of her neck turning cold and itchy. Why is she putting herself through this, on top of everything else? She thinks of the baby, of what the website had said about avoiding stress wherever possible.

'Fuck it.' She makes to dismount the pavement and drive off when the front door of 28 Saxon Way opens a crack and then swings wide open. There, framed by the roses that have been so lovingly tended since she was a child, stands her mum. She looks older. Smaller. She is wearing a large, heavy knit grey jumper that nestles cosily around her neck, over a pair of neat navy trousers. Her hair is pulled loosely back from her face. It looks greyer. Grey. Her face gives nothing away. She looks out to the car and Claudia realises she can't see who's in it through the tinted windows.

Claudia grabs her handbag and slides out of the driver's side before her flight mode kicks in again. The car flashes loudly as she locks it and she's overwhelmingly self-conscious of how ostentatious it looks. How flashy she looks in her designer clothes and her Mulberry tote bag.

'Hi, Mum.' Claudia weakly raises a hand as she

click-click-clicks on her heels towards her, then stops at the entrance to the garden, waiting to be invited in.

Her mum looks her up and down as if breathing her in. A beat. Two. Time stands still as the two women face each other. The weight of the unsaid, the years of silence, the anger, the hurt, it's like a palpable force field between them. Claudia cannot move. She can't turn to get back in the car or make towards her mother, who stands with her arms firmly folded across her chest.

And then, it shifts.

'Let's go in.' Her mum stands aside to let Claudia through the front door.

'So, do you want to tell me why you're here or should I guess?' her mum asks with her back to her, as she holds the just boiled kettle.

Claudia sighs and rubs her forehead. 'Do I have to have a reason?'

'No, of course not. It's just—' She stops mid-sentence, pours water over the teabags and goes to the fridge for the milk. 'It's just a surprise, Laudie. You've just surprised me. I thought it was a salesperson when I saw the car outside.'

'It's obscene, isn't it?' Claudia replies, accepting the mug from her mum and blowing before taking a grateful sip. 'It wasn't my choice, obviously.'

Her mum sits on the opposite side of the table. The kitchen looks exactly the same as when she was a child. The glass jars full of pasta and rice and dried pulses in neat rows on the shelf next to the cooker. The dated MDF kitchen cabinets, once the height of chic when first purchased decades ago. The framed pictures of the Peak District, rolling hills and dewy fields. The corkboard pinned with notes, shopping lists, cards, photographs of her as a child. The Robert Dyas radio on the window ledge that plays Radio 4 all day for company, from the moment her mum rises until she switches the lights off to go up to bed. The bowl of fruit in the centre of the kitchen table, filled with tangerines and Granny Smiths. Claudia reaches for one.

'Are you hungry? I can make you something if you are?' her mum asks, and Claudia retreats her hand.

'No. I'm fine. I'm happy with the tea.' She takes another sip.

A few moments pass in silence, before her mum asks, 'Laudie, you're not ill, are you?'

'No, God, no. Look, Mum, I know it's weird me

showing up like this. I know I should have come sooner, it's just—' She shrugs.

'OK. OK, well that will have to do for now.'

'Honestly, Mum, I'm not dying! I'm pregnant.'

A look ghosts across her mum's face. She resets it to a huge smile. 'Oh, my girl, that is such wonderful news. Such amazing news.' She pushes her chair back with a scrape and wraps her arms around her daughter, kissing the top of her head as Claudia buries her face into her jumper. 'That is such amazing news, it really is. How far gone are you?' She stands back to take in Claudia as if for the first time. Her eyes hungrily search her body for signs of change.

'Um, I don't know exactly. I think about six weeks. It's very early. I know you're meant to wait until twelve weeks but—'

'But nothing, I knew I was pregnant with you almost immediately.'

Her mum continues to hold her tightly and asks in a voice so quiet Claudia has to strain to hear it, 'Whatever has happened, you can tell me.'

Tears prick Claudia's eyes. She goes to speak but has lost her voice, so takes a sip of the water her mum has placed down on the table for her on a Van Gogh print coaster. Her mum sits on the chair opposite her and waits patiently for Claudia to respond.

Claudia rubs her eye sockets with the heels of her hands, bringing some relief to the pressure headache that has started to build.

'Are you in trouble?' her mum asks.

'No.' Claudia sniffs loudly and wipes her nose on the back of her hand. Her mum passes her a tissue that she has stuffed up her cardigan sleeve; it smells of Elizabeth Arden's Red Door.

'No, not me.'

'Is it Simon?' Her mum takes Claudia's hands in hers, squeezing them tightly and asking again, 'What happened?'

'I don't know where to start.'

'The beginning is always a good place?' her mum suggests.

'He's been arrested for embezzlement.'

Her mum nods for her to continue and Claudia knows that she has come to the right place. That she is safe to talk. That her mum will put the past to one side for now to protect her at all costs, both her and the baby.

'What happened?' she asks again.

'The police came to the house with a warrant. They've taken his computer and laptop as evidence.'

'But what is he being accused of?' her mum presses further.

Claudia exhales slowly. 'They say he has been using the company's money to fund highly sensitive and politically dubious businesses worldwide.' Claudia takes a sip of her tea. Her voice quivers but her hands are now stoic.

A silence falls between them. Her mum smooths down the creases in the tablecloth with the flat of her hand.

'Why?' she finally asks.

'I don't know. What drives anyone to do anything, Mum? I'm just hoping it's one big misunderstanding.'

'I mean,' and her mum reaches for Claudia's hand, holding it firmly, 'what have you done?'

Claudia tries to take another sip of her tea but her throat has dried up, making it impossible to swallow.

Her mum raises an eyebrow in response. 'You may be an amazing actress, Laudie, but you are also my daughter. You can't fool me.'

Claudia puts down her mug. She stands and heads to the window. Two blackbirds are eating from the feeder, yellow beaks pecking at the peanuts. The garden is in hibernation at the moment but in a few weeks' time the first shoots of spring will start to push their way through the soil.

Claudia, caught somewhere between relief and fear, cannot bring herself to speak. Once she starts to talk, it will be out in the world. For now, it is simply one of many possibilities that may or may not have happened. An avenue that even the most accomplished barrister would be hesitant to pursue. Her and Simon have an unbreakable bond. They smile for the press but keep their private lives just that: private. They are likable. Effortless. Photogenic. Their faces adorn the covers of glossy magazines.

'Laudie? You have to trust me.'

'I do,' Claudia whispers, 'it's not that.'

THE FIRST MESSAGE exchange she had seen between Simon and Susie had pinged up on her iPad. For a man who made his fortune online, it seemed a cruel twist of fate that his affair should be exposed because he had synced all their devices. Looking back, she kicked herself for not noticing anything beforehand. The quick exchange of glances, the relaxed manner with which Susie spoke to her employer. How she had changed her hair, her clothes, her perfume. Claudia didn't blame her. She knew how manipulative Simon could be, morphing women into the image of what slotted into the life he had created. She herself should know; when she looks down at her implants, she knows her bosoms will soon change shape again, but this time naturally, as her baby grows.

She didn't want to punish Susie, however much the thought of her betrayal hurt her. They were never friends, but they were both women, and that had to count for something. But Simon knew what he was doing. He always has. He stopped loving Claudia a long time ago, she sees that now. He viewed her as a commodity. And like the systems he works with, he had decided to go for an upgrade.

The paper trail of embezzlement was easy enough to orchestrate if you knew his passwords, which she did, as he wrote them in his ideas book, which he kept next to his bed to capture those middle-of-the-night moments of inspiration for the 'next big thing'. Stupid man.

She syphoned regular but differing amounts into offshore accounts, so as not to raise suspicion from the company. She changed numerous personal standing orders to come from his company credit card. She was careful, so careful. Nothing too big, but combined, hugely damaging for his business and his reputation. Orchestrating his downfall just as he had slowly chipped away at her sense of worth over the years. A screen grab of where the money was going, sent to the police, was all it took, forwarded from an anonymous email address she had set up in an internet café.

The request for her to come in to make an official statement was left unanswered, but she knew she had started the domino effect. The empire he had built would slowly start to crumble in front of him, like a sandcastle when the tide comes in.

'CAN WE STAY HERE TONIGHT?' Claudia asks. The shift from 'I' to 'we' has been a natural transition, and she rests her hand once again on her stomach.

'Your old room is made up,' her mum says. 'I hope you know what you're doing, Laudie.'

Claudia sighs, her breath ragged in her throat. Just then, her ears prick as she hears a familiar name on the radio. She stands with a jolt and turns it up.

'… arrested outside his house. Multi-millionaire Simon Peterson has earned his fortune through online investments—'

Claudia turns the radio off. The press have been

quick to respond. She only tipped them off less than an hour ago.

'They're going to want to talk to you,' her mum says.

'I know. I told them I'll be here. That I need to be with my mum.'

Her mum goes to reach for her hand again but changes her mind at the last moment and picks up her empty mug, taking it to the sink.

Claudia has thought through everything she needs to say to make a conviction stick, while maintaining her ignorance of all the comings and goings, but she can't be complacent. She needs to remember her lines, to act the part of the loving wife, shocked and devastated by her husband's actions.

The doorbell rings. Claudia can see the outline of a policeman's hat through the frosted glass. Her mum wipes her hands on a tea towel; Claudia notices they are shaking.

'Thank you,' she mouths, before her mum heads towards the front door.

This will be the greatest performance of Claudia's life.

She closes her eyes, breathes in through her nose, pursing her lips then stretching them wide as she's done countless times before a performance.

'Yes, Officer, she's in the kitchen. We're both in shock, to be honest,' her mum says, confidently playing her own role.

'Show time,' Claudia whispers under her breath, as a tear rolls down her cheek.

ANNA JEFFERSON IS a playwright and author. She has published two novels, *Winging It* (2020) and *Nailing It* (2021), and is currently working on her third book. Anna lives in Brighton with her husband and two children. She is represented by United Agents.

annajefferson.co.uk

Twitter: @annajefferson

Insta: @annajeffersonauthor

THE LUCKY ONES

ROSIE WALKER

I scan each face in the courtroom today, but no one meets my eyes. Except one.

I had a favourite news reporter, Graham Fallow. They stationed him in front of the police incident tape at all my fires, facing the camera with a cold-blushed nose and visible breath. He spoke into a microphone as they wheeled out the bodies or doused the damp remains of the smoking buildings.

We were connected, Graham and me. It was as if I had his phone number. By setting these fires, I was calling him. I imagined his landline ringing at 3am – 'Graham, there's been another fire' – and him dragged from his warm bed to stand in the street all night. Tartan scarf tucked into his black overcoat, bleary eyes. Talking about me. Performing for the camera in the street where I'd stood just a couple of hours before.

He said my patterns were illogical and without reason. A linear pattern, for instance, could indicate a delivery driver, probably with a criminal record. Mapped clusters of activity would suggest the fire setter was operating in his own area, near where he lived. They could detect no pattern when they mapped *my* fires.

How did I decide who were the lucky ones, and who were not? I didn't use a rule book. But sometimes it seemed as if I already knew them. As if *they* chose *me*.

Like Andy.

I was walking home through a part of Edinburgh where the wynds were so narrow that the buildings seemed to conspire overhead. My footsteps echoed under the dripping railway bridge. The drizzle slowly soaked into my woollen jumper, rekindling the musky trace of a previous fire that was trapped between its thick fibres. I raised my sleeve to my nose to inhale the faint scent of scorched wood and closed my eyes. It had been a long day.

A man walked towards me, pushing a beautiful mountain bike, shiny and black, with disc brakes. Young, with a dimple on one cheek. Mud-spattered shorts. I stepped aside to let him past on the narrow pavement and he looked up at me, nodded his thanks. He had a nice smile. I could imagine the expression on his face when he came home from a ride, dirty and happy.

I liked him immediately. We could easily be friends. Perhaps his name was Andy.

As his footsteps began to fade, I turned back and followed him, back under the bridge, back towards the city, back where I'd come from. I followed slowly, keeping a long distance behind him and making little noise. Ducking into wynds and avoiding the orange pools of streetlights. I listened to his purposeful strides on the wet cobbles through the Old Town, his shoes making a delightful crunching sound on the gritted ground.

From across the road I watched him lock his bike and open his tenement door. Through the window I saw him switch on the lights and throw his keys into the bowl on the hall table. It was a nice flat on the ground floor, small and cosy. A coat rack, a hallway rug, a mirror on the wall. I'd like to live somewhere like that one day.

He didn't close the curtains. I could see him facing the kitchen window, washing pots in the sink. Eventually I renewed my walk home, now doubled in distance. I wanted to meet Andy. I told myself that I would see him at least one more time.

Sometimes he closed the curtains as soon as the light faded, but other nights he'd forget and I could watch him. I watched him living and breathing, talking and laughing with someone. Probably his wife or girlfriend. Lucky girl. She didn't deserve him.

I saw them watching television; I saw the girl cooking dinner. Andy helped her. I think I even saw them arguing once.

I imagined he was my friend. That we debated

the nationalisation of our railways; arabica versus robusta coffee; mountain or road bikes. These discussions would be heated, but we'd always agree to differ in the end. Then we'd toast to our individual tastes. He'd drink Islay, I'd have Speyside.

I chose him. He was perfect. He was mine.

One night, I was wandering along his street as he returned home from work. It was meant to be. As before, I caught his eye; he noticed me. He felt the same connection I did.

'Hello there,' I whispered.

He smiled and looked back down at the pavement, continuing on his way.

'I said, hello,' I called, louder this time.

His footsteps slowed. He turned his head but didn't stop walking. 'Hi,' he mumbled into his coat collar, turned up against the rain.

'Nice evening, isn't it?'

He nodded and walked on, turned through his gate, chained his bike and stepped into his house.

He closed his front door.

The lock's metallic *thunk* echoed through the stairwell.

My hands balled into fists in my pockets. My body shook all over.

We should be friends. How could he ignore our connection?

I waited until I couldn't wait any more. I crossed the road and strode up the path. I stroked the saddle of his bicycle with my fingertips as I walked past. My one mistake.

The rest was simple. Pour petrol under the door, hold it there with an old towel, strike a match. It's the vapours that burn, not the liquid itself. I stood motionless on Andy's front path, watching the flames lick up the door. Through the lighted window, they lounged on the sofa. She was reading a book; he was watching television.

He was still mine.

The fire caught quickly, as if it felt my anger; the fire and I were one being. My whole body vibrated with frustration and excitement. Soon, the flames were licking the leaves of the tree in the garden. A branch set alight, and flaming leaves broke free, soaring into the air like hundreds of miniature phoenixes.

There was so much fire. I wanted to dance around the flames – in the street, in the garden. I wanted to tear off my clothes to feel the heat and light of the flames on my naked flesh. I wanted to run into the flames and let them claim me as their own. I wanted my hair to crumple and singe. I wanted to breathe it all in, smoke and fire, until I burned from the inside out. I wanted it all.

When I raised my fingers to my nose I could smell the glory. Petrol, matches, charred wood, smoke, fire. I slipped my fingers into my mouth and sucked, sucked, sucked them clean. I tasted the fire, licked it right off each one of my blackened fingers.

I wanted to stand there all night to see things develop. I could have stayed forever, watching my fires. But I had to tear myself away.

The view wasn't particularly good from my car. But people are quick to call the fire brigade in those quieter parts of the city, and the police are never far behind. At my peak, the police often arrived before the fire service. They were so desperate to catch me.

I allowed myself to use my windscreen wipers so I could see the flames. I opened the windows to smell the smoke. I thought I could see a figure in the window of the house, banging on the glass. I was glad to see Andy again. I liked him. I'd made the right choice.

My hands shook with excitement, so it was hard to get a firm grasp on the handbrake. Still staring at the house, I let the car roll slowly, watching the flames grow as I moved closer. Orange and red, flickering through the darkened car window. I always choose night-time. Flames look better at night.

When the best was over, I drove home. *Fled the*

scene, as Graham would say. My flat was cold and empty, but I could detect a faint tang of stale smoke hiding in the folds of all my clothes. I breathed it in until I felt my lungs could burst.

I switched on the local news, and there was Graham, standing outside the house. *Breaking news here in the outskirts of Edinburgh tonight: police have found two bodies in the remains of a burnt out home. Early investigations indicate that this could be the work of a serial fire-raiser.*

I thought I could see a faint smile as he talked about what I had done. A kindred spirit, perhaps. Me, a serial fire-raiser. I liked to hear him say that. I wanted to hear him say that again.

Sometimes I would wait up all night to see the reports of my fires. I recorded all the news reports onto VHS, cataloguing the videos on shelves, arranged chronologically. I wrote the date, time and address on the label with a black marker pen, and I added a red dot to signify the lucky ones: a dot for each life taken. From the footage, I learned the names of the people involved. People who should have been my friends, in a different world.

I didn't struggle when they finally arrested me. It was exciting; now I'd get to tell everyone about my fires. People would ask me questions and they'd write about me in the newspapers. I could talk, and people would listen. People would want to be my friend.

I still think about my fires. They're all catalogued in my head, just as they were on my video shelf. When I can't get to sleep, I review all my fires in order, one by one. I start with the first, the breakthrough fire, and remember all the details: the smells, the sounds, what burned, what didn't. Who died, who didn't. And why I chose each house for a burning.

Today, I scan each face in the courtroom, wondering who they are. Mothers, brothers, children belonging to the people I selected. They look at me with hatred, but none of them can meet my eyes, except one.

Graham, my news reporter, sits in the front row. He sees me looking at him, as if he's been waiting for me to find him. He grins at me, giving a slight nod of his head.

We could easily be friends.

ROSIE WALKER IS the author of two novels, *The House Fire* (2022) and *Secrets of a Serial Killer* (2020), both published by HarperCollins UK's One More Chapter and available in print, ebook and audio.

She lives in Edinburgh, Scotland with her husband, daughter and dog. She is currently working on her third novel.

rosiejanewalker.com

Twitter: @ciderwithrosie

Instagram: @rosiejanewalker

Facebook: @rosiewalkerauthor

HAVING IT ALL

GILLIAN HARVEY

The dinner came up in almost regimental order. First the profiteroles: the thick, syrupy chocolate; cream; a chewed, barely-recognisable ball of flour and butter. Then the beef wellington – the best in London apparently – wetly clinging to the porcelain, garnished with carrots.

It was enough. She dragged her hand across her mouth and stood up, unsteady in her heels. Saliva clung to her wrist. It was brown, chocolate-stained. The other cubicles were quiet. Towards the end of the row she could hear the dainty sound of someone peeing. She unlocked the door and looked out at the small, tiled sink area. It was empty. Taking her chance, she slipped her body – in its £2,000 Donna Karan dress – out of the cubicle door, and walked to the sink, her Chanel heels clipping on the floor.

Leaning on the porcelain, she looked at herself, her mouth a smudged line of red. Her eyes were slightly bloodshot. Knuckles a tell-tale red: Russell's sign, they called it. She turned on the tap.

'Atta girl,' she heard the echo of her father's voice in her mind. Two years too late to make him proud, but maybe somehow he knew anyway. She hated all that speculation about afterlife – had no time for religion – but since the man who'd doted on her had passed, she'd found herself wondering.

Her mother's voice was only too prevalent. 'Women can't have it all,' she'd warned when she'd heard Ally's ambition to run for mayor. 'Not really. Some just look like they do.' Ally hadn't known what her mum had meant then. But she did now.

Watching the faces of her sleeping kids under feather duvets and feeling the rush of love that only seemed to come when they were unconscious, she'd felt it. She was a mother, yet not a mother. She loved the idea of them; she loved them – in an abstract, detached kind of way. But she wasn't close to them. Not like Jake, with his hide-and-seek, bubble battles and the ridiculous drama he made of bedtime stories. It was him they ran to when they were hurt. His arms they sought, even when she stood there waiting to hold them.

'Where does it end, Ally?' he'd said to her tonight, his back rigid, his hands in the washing up bowl, covered in suds. 'What do you wanna do? Run the country?'

'Maybe,' she'd said, partly to annoy him. 'Maybe I want to rule the whole damn world. Why does that bother you so much?'

It had been unfair, she thought, pulling a stray hair back into place. He'd always supported her. Never felt emasculated by her success. She'd known what he'd meant: he wanted more of her; the children needed more of her. Her career was taking her away from the family – weekends, evenings, calls in the middle of the night she couldn't ignore.

'It's for them,' she'd said then, into the angry silence. It's all for them.'

'But—'

'It's to make a better world. I can't just stand there while this country goes to the dogs.'

'And they're just a sacrifice you have to make, I guess.'

She'd left, then. Her car – sleek, with its blacked-out windows – had been waiting outside. She'd wanted him to come at first, but the sitter had been busy and he'd said he didn't mind. Now she wondered whether he'd engineered it. Leaving her to stand alone for the photos – her best smile, no man on her arm. It wasn't a good look. Her voters were all about family values. But tonight it wouldn't matter. She'd won and she'd get the image right by next time. Jake would come around. He always came around.

A cubicle creaked and a blond-haired woman stepped out into the sink area.

'Great night,' she said, washing her hands vigorously under the tap. 'I love your dress.'

'Thank you.'

'Congratulations.'

Ally smiled as the woman hastily drew her hands through the hot air of the dryer and clipped towards the door. 'See you out there.'

'Yes, won't be a sec.'

She turned off the tap, shaking droplets from her hands and using the rest to smooth her fringe. Reaching into her handbag, she pulled out a concealer and dabbed it under her eyes, covering the stubborn grey bags, and at the corners of her mouth, which were cracked and raw. She looked good. She always looked good afterwards; the effort made her eyes sparkle.

'You see what you want and you don't quit till you get it.' Dad's voice again. He'd understood. 'Our family, we don't quit. Hamiltons do not quit.'

'Hamiltons don't quit,' she said to herself softly, looking at her own blank expression.

She didn't want to quit – not the early morning exercise, the breakfast meetings; quit being the one people came to, the person with the answers. Her morning coffee and croissant brought to her desk. The papers. Issues. Fights to take on. She didn't want to quit on Grace or Abigail, or Jake. The softness of the girls' skin when she leaned over their beds for a too-late goodnight kiss. The complete and utter surrender of their tiny bodies to sleep.

Their tousled hair in the morning as they ate their cereal and argued over cartoons.

Her fingers still smelled vaguely of vomit. She rubbed hand cream into them vigorously, then put the cap back on the bottle and slipped it into her clutch. It would have to do. She drew breath, feeling less wobbly now, shook back her hair and made for the exit.

'Great party.' A man smiled as she crossed the floor. 'And congratulations on your win.'

'Thank you,' she smiled as graciously as she could manage. 'I can't wait to get started.'

***

GILLIAN HARVEY IS AN AUTHOR, columnist and freelance writer who lives in France with her husband Ray and their five children. Her latest book, *A Year at the French Farmhouse*, was published in September 2022 by Boldwood Books.

gillianharvey.com

THE TEARS OF VENUS

VICTORIA AND DELILAH DOWD

There has only ever been space in Jane Fullerby's heart for Bastet. Bassie has been the biggest part of Jane's life for almost two decades. An unhealthily long time, or so the local gossips would have it. But Bassie has no care for what people say. She's a cat. A Siamese with a cold eye for everyone. Her life revolves around the next meal and a doleful existence, both of which are profusely provided by Miss Fullerby. She shares everything with her – food, her bed, even her thoughts.

For the bird-like woman, her greatest hope is that her modest fortune will go with Bassie. It is the only way Jane can guarantee a nice little cortege of greedy mourners all willing to provide a more than comfortable life for whatever remaining years this malign, old creature may have. Her only concern is that Bassie is taken care of. In exchange, they will receive a not inconsiderable sum of money. And, of course, the greatest prize – the large double sapphire ring Jane Fullerby wears. A family heirloom, passed down like a disorder.

The ring has a far more important name than its owner. The Tears of Venus are said to be the first tears shed by the goddess when she was born from a shell into the arms of the ocean. Or at least that's what Jane's mother told her. Venus beheld the beauty of its salt waves for the very first time and wept. Fortunately, there must have been a jeweller on hand to preserve these fine specimens and place them in this glorious, ornate setting. Although Jane's mother was vague on the mechanics of such an endeavour. When Jane was just twenty, her mother died on the same day as Queen Victoria, which somehow seemed to add credence to the jewel's story as it passed to her hand. Now Jane is the last Fullerby and has no one to leave it to except Bassie and whoever takes her into their care.

The stones themselves are an unreal, toxic blue that no one would ever wish to swim in. Beauty seems to be a peculiar term for them. In contrast to their meek host, they glow with an acid light deep within, as if slowly leeching all the electricity from their wearer's frail frame. There is an undeniable, hypnotic quality to the cut of this ring, with the suggestion that to stare too long might lead to some irreparably blighted life unfolding for the viewer. It's nothing so dramatic as a curse. That's not subtle enough for this ring. But there's a definite hint of insistent bad luck lingering over it. Supposedly born of love, its beguiling sheen leans more towards a possessive nature than any other form of romance. A more sinister, obsessive love.

It's a morbid January morning and Bassie

languishes on her window ledge, watching Sebastian Lessing's carefully planned approach. This one is noticeably younger than the fifty-seven-year-old lady he is about to set about capturing. The suitor stalks down the leaf-littered path, an ungracious, keen edge to each step. Just how Bassie's owner is not able to see the avarice bleeding out of every pore of this man, she doesn't even consider. She's a cat.

Jane opens the door with the kind of insipid whey-face that suggests opportunity to this breed of man. If he were to be sliced open, he would have charm written all the way through his spine. As he bows, the enchantment breathes out of him in a great cloud over Jane Fullerby. She had begun to think her days of being alluring to men were over, but as he grips her hand and lets his face linger before kissing it, she feels the promise of love travel up through her fingers. The kind that embeds itself like a fishhook.

He, too, is of course instantly enraptured in that moment as he holds her delicate hand and stares into the cold-blue depths of those jewels.

Tea and compliments follow.

'What a delightful home you have, Miss Fullerby.'

A blush.

'Such exquisite taste.'

A coy smile.

'Oh, and who is this?'

Sebastian peers closely at Bassie but keeps his hands firmly clenched behind his back. 'Aren't you *magnificent*?'

Bassie does not answer. She's a cat.

Jane's fate is sealed. The courtship is short-lived. Sebastian's regard for the timid lady is as thin as the wedding veil, her happiness as fleeting as the flowers in her bouquet. He is quick to abandon her in favour of her money and, more importantly, finding new ways to spend it. She tells herself it's just love at a different density to before. But his management of her neglect is meticulous, invading every part of her existence like a tree with too many roots. He controls every aspect of her life with precision. Where she goes – nowhere. What she eats – very little. What she drinks – a tonic he prepares. He blames her for losing things. She has become forgetful, she'll admit that. But things seem to go missing all the time, particularly a few days before another of his card games. Sometimes immediately after as well. Finally, even the ring itself disappears.

'But I wouldn't have lost it! I couldn't,' she pleads. 'I would never do such a thing.'

'Oh, so you are suggesting something else

happened to the ring, are you?' His face is white fury. 'I see! You are trying to blame me. This is too much, even for you!'

That night she weeps dry tears. She is scared this time.

She grows weak, depleted by loneliness, she assumes. Jane is often ill now; her sickly bouts increase, her limbs ache and her eyesight fails. She can barely move, her legs atrophy, as if they are stuffed with straw, words are difficult to find and even harder to speak. Her mouth is all but sewn shut. She wishes she could say it. Speak it out loud. Say bloodstained pillows. Say moulting. But she is becoming no more than a hollowed model of herself.

Her husband calls a specialist doctor he has found, who can offer no reason, save for the fact that perhaps the lady might be overly anxious about health issues. 'In the profession, we call it "hypochondria".' She has, as her husband says, always been of a nervous disposition. Jane knows she is abandoned. She knows this will not last much longer. She comforts herself with the knowledge that she has her cat to share everything with, even her melancholy. But she also knows this can't be for long. Her beloved cat is so old.

Bassie dies on an autumn morning as she

watches the leaves falling through a low saffron sun. Light pools on her window ledge as if the rays of heaven are gathering up her soul. Or, at least, that's what Jane tells her unmoved husband.

'I shall call for the taxidermist and have her preserved for eternity.' She avoids the word *stuffed*.

He sighs, deep in the knowledge that this will all be over soon. 'As you wish.' He remains unimpressed. 'I have business in town this evening. I won't return until the morning.' Her husband admires himself in the long hallway mirror that must be growing tired of his reflection. She does not care to ask what business involves spending so much and earning nothing.

When Sebastian has gone, the house breathes out a sigh of relief and relaxes into its mourning. Bassie lies still in her usual place. She doesn't look at Jane anymore. She is a dead cat.

When the last image is firmly burnt into the back of her eyes, it is time to let go. The taxidermist, Mr Summeridge, is as kind and humble as an undertaker. He asks some questions about positioning and look.

'I try to capture a little of their … essence in all my creations. A little of the life they once had.' He carries with him a folder of his creations, detailing the menagerie of creatures all preserved in their moment of death. 'These all live in my workshop now.'

The clouded outlines that she can make out through her weary eyes confuse her. She frowns. 'Tell me, do they not wish to claim their beloved pets?'

He gives a sad smile. 'Not everyone is as appreciative of my work as you, dear lady. Not everyone in a house loves the pets whilst they are alive, so their bodies hold no interest for them after death. If an owner passes away, sometimes the rest of the family do not wish to keep the preserved pet. But nor do they feel comfortable simply throwing it away. Often, they return it to me.'

Her mind flicks to Sebastian. She imagines him taking great delight in disposing of Bassie, an empty-hearted smile of satisfaction cutting across his face.

'Ah,' she says ruefully, 'I fear my husband is more likely to throw Bassie into the bin once I am gone.'

Mr Summeridge looks troubled and glances down at the posed animal.

They discuss the details and arrangements. Mr Summeridge is sensitive and respectful, two words Jane has grown unaccustomed to.

The next few weeks without Bassie in the house

seem wrong. Disjointed. Time concertinas in and out with long hours of grief, then whole afternoons lost in a mindless blur.

Sebastian is not present. There is that to be grateful for, at least.

When Jane next sees Bassie, the cat is no more than a mounted shell of skin filled with straw and tow, with glassy eyes screwed into her skull. Mr Summeridge prefers the old, traditional techniques, he tells her. But Bassie doesn't care. She is a dead, stuffed cat.

Jane, however, does care. She cares very much. Her Bassie is back. Jane is as exuberant as her frail features will permit. She still has a watered down look about her, but her wistful pleasure is clear to the taxidermist. He has done his job. This is one of the most precious moments of his work and if he could preserve *that* look, he would.

She shakes Mr Summeridge's hand sincerely and he bows.

'You have brought meaning back.' Tears clean her eyes. 'You are a magician! You have brought her back to life for me.'

The man stoops again. 'If my skill brings happiness …'

'Oh, beyond compare!'

She speaks to her rigid pet. 'We will put you

back where you belong.' She places Bassie on her usual window ledge. Viewed through Jane's hazy eyes, the afternoon sunlight casts the cat in a poignant light as she stares out again over her view. Bassie, of course, doesn't care. She is a dead, stuffed cat.

Later, after tea, Mr Summeridge leaves Jane to the contemplation of his work.

Sebastian doesn't even notice the animal watching his return home up the path. He only sees the cat when he passes the window ledge in Jane's bedroom, but his dislike is instant.

He recoils. 'Filthy creature. This will bring bad luck, no doubt.'

Every time Sebastian passes the window after that he gives a derisive glance. But Bassie can't see him. She faces out to the world just as she has always done.

However, Sebastian's prediction comes to fruition much quicker than they could have imagined and their luck does indeed take an almost immediate turn for the worse. Money evaporates as fast as Sebastian can spend it at the card tables. He is barely home to see Jane's health deteriorate – more romantic souls might say from a neglected heart.

As the year fades out, so too does Bassie. Her

fur grows thin and patchy, riddled with the moths that plague the house. The balding, dry flesh is visible below.

Jane seems to mirror her pet's descent. Her own skin is as grey and soft as ash. The cotton-white wisps of her hair are barely distinguishable against the pillowcase as she lies dying. If she was left in the fog she would have looked like a ghost, a shot of paling silver against the darkness. Her breath is no more than a thin tendril when she whispers her cat's name one last time. 'Bassie.'

Sebastian raises a greying eyebrow and watches her die.

The widower rips through the house with the speed of new life, sweeping away clothes, paintings and ornaments. Some things are sold, some given away. Bassie, however, fulfils her owner's suggestion. Sebastian hurls the tattered beast into the bin. But by this point, old and decrepit, with her mistress gone, Bassie doesn't care. She is, after all, nothing more than a dead, mounted cat that nobody wants.

Only that isn't true. Somebody does want her. Mr Summeridge performs his solemn duty and embarks upon a night-time salvage mission.

The taxidermist lifts Bassie from amongst the vegetable peelings and the remains of her owner's belongings. He places the dirty, stuffed animal in a box and walks away.

He has fulfilled his promise.

Back in his shop, Mr Summeridge carefully lifts Bastet out and places her on the counter. He does not put the cat on the shelf with all the other discarded animals, however. Not yet. He will take the perished animal to the police, first thing tomorrow, as Jane instructed. He is unsure why, but having seen the fast necrosis and balding of its owner, he can guess. He nods gravely at the animal as if he can see the wretched lady in its eyes. The lady who knew her fate was sealed and continued to share everything with her beloved, old cat.

There is one more job to perform for Bastet's mistress.

He carefully prises out the creature's eyes, leaving only blind, hollow sockets. The poor, beleaguered animal, a once proud Siamese, is brought so low and looks even more pitiful and lost. But in the dusty workshop light, Mr Summeridge holds up two perfect sapphires. They were exactly where Jane had told him they would be. She had said they were beautiful beyond compare but he had not imagined such magnificence. She'd also said her greatest hope was that her fortune would go with whoever took care of Bastet. Her wish has been granted.

Mr Summeridge places the more usual glass eyes into the holes. He cannot leave the lady blind.

The Times

On 5th November 1938 Mr Sebastian Lessing was sentenced to be hanged for the murder of his wife, Mrs Jane Lessing.

After it was confirmed that her cat had died from ingestion of meadow saffron (Colchicum autumnale), Mrs Lessing's body was exhumed and large quantities of the poison were found in her system.

The plant, more commonly known as 'naked ladies', was found growing extensively at their home and Mr Lessing was in possession of a large jar of the dried stamens which both the maid and the cook had seen him administer in the form of a tonic to Mrs Lessing.

The victim had unwittingly shared this tonic with her cat. It proved to be Mr Lessing's undoing when a local taxidermist, tasked with preserving the remains, noticed unusual levels of decay and hair loss in the animal's preserved remains after he salvaged it from a nearby bin.

VICTORIA DOWD IS the award-winning author of the bestselling Smart Woman's Mystery series. Her debut novel, *The Smart Woman's Guide to Murder*, won The People's Book Prize for fiction 2021 and was named In Search of the Classic Mystery Novel's Book of the Year 2020. Victoria was awarded the Gothic Fiction prize for her short fiction. Originally from Yorkshire, she was a criminal defence barrister for many years. **Delilah Dowd** is her daughter and also a published, award-winning author.

victoriadowd.com

Twitter: @victoria_dowd

Facebook: @v.dowdauthor

TREASURE

HOLLY RACE

K elly felt about her ex-mother-in-law's death the way some people felt about Thatcher's. *Ding dong the witch is dead!* What she said to her daughter upon hearing the news, though, was, 'She was a very strong woman. We need more of those in the world, not less.'

'She was a cunt, mum,' Leah replied. 'I wish you'd stop trying to be all feminist about it.'

And they had gone back to cutting mushrooms for their carbonara, accompanied by the sounds of Katy Perry's *Roar*, which was as modern as Kelly could bear and not so old-fashioned that Leah would pretend to shrivel of old age upon hearing it.

Kelly often worried that she wasn't a good feminist. She found herself worrying that Leah needed the influence of her father more than she got; that she'd go off the rails with just her around. She masturbated to thoughts of her ex dominating her in ways he had never done when they were married. Mostly, she wished she wasn't having to do this alone. She had worked her head off to forge the camaraderie between herself and Leah through the difficult pre-teen years following her divorce from Justin. Now they were safely in the teenager phase, and Kelly was satisfied to see that Leah reserved all of her hormonal angst for her father.

It was the two of them against the world, against that family, and it was all Kelly had.

'I hope they don't give me one of the big bedrooms,' Leah said as they pulled up to the Hall's forecourt.

'Well at least I didn't raise a gold digger,' Kelly replied.

'I'm totally a gold digger. But if they shove me in a big bedroom it'll only be a guilt thing.'

Kelly was grateful that she'd never had to live in Northfield Hall itself. When she and Justin were married, they'd stayed in a newly converted barn on the grounds of the estate – at her insistence. It had been her only red line when they'd got engaged, and the only one Justin had been firm about with his mother – the not living with her in the Hall. She could remember Evelyn's face when Justin had told her. The streaming tears, the exclamations that she was going to be all alone, the way the monkey pendant she always wore glinted against her breastbone.

'I wish you wouldn't forget your mother,' she had wailed, and the ruby eyes in the monkey's solid form had glittered strangely in the light of the chandeliers.

Northfield Hall had its own marker on Google Maps, although it had never been open to the public – a matter of pride to Evelyn. She didn't have to thank the plebs for paying the heating bill. The mansion, built by plantation owners, with its Georgian pillars and smooth, butter stone, sat on a hill just outside Bath. When Justin had first shown Kelly round the place, the day she met Evelyn of the pursed lips, Kelly had thought how difficult it must be to live in such a place, let alone grow up there as Justin had done. Not being able to shout down to your other half to bring you a tea because they wouldn't be able to hear you from so far away. Having a separate room for watching TV and reading a book, as though the two didn't go hand in hand, or foot on lap, on the same sofa.

No wonder Justin was so strange and intriguing when she met him. No wonder she spent so many years trying to uncover the riddle of him.

He was waiting at the top of the steps when they pulled up, his suit immaculate but his hair as unruly as ever. Kelly wondered whether Abigail, his new(ish) wife, liked scraping her nails through it as much as Kelly had done.

'I'd have paid for a taxi,' he said, coming down the steps and joining them as Leah got out of the car. He folded her into a hug. Kelly remained in the driver's seat, waiting for her daughter to close the passenger door.

'I wanted Mum to drop me off,' Leah said. 'I'm sorry, Dad.'

Justin leant down to peer through the open door. 'Would you like to come, Kels?'

'I'm not wearing black,' Kelly said.

'You know I don't mind about that stuff.'

Evelyn would have minded, Kelly thought, and suddenly the idea of attending didn't seem so awful.

'Could you, Mum?' Leah asked, suddenly vulnerable. Leah would always be the unhelpful reminder of Justin's first marriage in that family, no matter how much Abigail tried to mask her feelings.

'If you're sure there are going to be enough sandwiches,' Kelly said, already getting out of the car.

'Come on, you can dance on her grave once everyone's gone,' Justin said.

Kelly linked arms with Leah, catching Justin's eyes flick over their joining and away again. He looked different to how she'd imagined he would. She thought he would be destroyed by his mother's death. They had been inseparable during Evelyn's life; he was always the undisputed favourite of her five children, the rest all girls and he the youngest and only boy. Evelyn only had to tell him how high to jump and he'd jump higher. For a while, Kelly had thought that there would be room for her. She had thought that his prioritising of his mother would translate into prioritising their own family.

But Justin didn't look broken or devastated. He looked free. Almost happy. It was infuriating and curious and Kelly almost felt sorry for Evelyn. She found it distasteful – she had never pegged Justin as someone who'd butter up his mother just for the inheritance, but that's what it looked like, after all. She glimpsed a chain nestling under his shirt collar. Was it? Kelly bet it was – the pendant, the golden monkey sitting upright, one paw raised to show that it held a clear, perfectly cut ruby. The only possession Evelyn had treasured more was Justin. It seemed like an odd choice, and on today of all days. Kelly had never pegged him as a jewellery wearer either.

The funeral was held in the Norman church that abutted, and had once been part of, the family estate. Kelly stayed at the back, and instead of feeling triumphant, as she had ever since Leah had told her that Evelyn had passed away, she felt a flooding sense of futility. What was the point, Evelyn? she wanted to ask the body in the walnut coffin. You pulled us apart. What now? Was it worth it?

As everyone filed back to the house, Kelly decided against the temptation of the sandwiches.

The Hall was haunted for her, its chandeliers dripping in scorn. There wouldn't be any satisfaction in going inside. So Kelly waited in the car, pretending to read her book, until Leah emerged from the house, ran down the steps and virtually threw herself into the passenger seat.

'That bad, huh?' Kelly said.

'You have no idea. Let's go.'

But as she drove, Kelly realised that, for the first time, Leah was hiding something from her. It was a new and uncomfortable feeling. Something about the off-handed way Leah answered her questions. The way she held herself a little aloof. An argument with her father? Kelly didn't know how to react or get the truth from her. When they got home, Leah pushed their dog, Scribble, to one side and slipped up to her room with an excuse so bald that Kelly almost laughed.

The truth came the next day. It started with a phone call. It was Justin, calling far too early, and she didn't answer it. But her stomach twisted. Another notch that told her that something had happened yesterday at Evelyn's wake. So after Leah clomped off to school, Kelly did the unthinkable. She snooped.

Leah's room wasn't stereotypical for a sixteen-year-old girl. It wasn't overly messy, and there were equal numbers of mother-daughter photos as there were photos of her with her friends. The windowsill was covered in seedlings, but Kelly knew exactly where to look. The vanity case that had once been Kelly's grandmother's – the only valuable family item she was able to pass down to her daughter.

It was sitting on the top shelf, the red velvet beneath it even tattier by comparison. The monkey's tiny ruby eyes glittered strangely at Kelly. Her phone buzzed in her pocket again. She didn't have to look at it to know it was Justin. Her first instinct was to wonder how she could fix this. Justin knew that Leah had stolen his mother's most treasured possession. He must do. She had worked so hard to try to maintain Leah's relationship with her father, even though he now had a new wife and young children, even though Leah had nevertheless taken sides in the clearest way possible by refusing joint custody. Kelly had been silently triumphant but had tried so hard not to show it. And now this. What would Justin do?

Scribble ran into the room and began humping Kelly's leg as she picked up the necklace and studied the detail up close. It was so beautiful, in a cold manner, much like Evelyn. The humping continued.

'Oh for heaven's sake, Scribble,' Kelly snapped. 'I wish – just lie down!'

Scribble slunk away, chastened. Something moved beneath Kelly's feet. A wobble, a glitch that made her stumble. Then it was gone.

'Did you feel that earthquake?' Kelly asked her colleagues later. The monkey necklace hung heavily around her neck. It was the kind of shape that should sway or roll from side to side as she moved, but it didn't; it stayed still against her breastbone, as though the monkey was on guard.

Her phone buzzed again. Another missed call from Justin. Another voicemail. Kelly checked the time – nearly Leah's lunch break.

'Another request for July,' Kelly's assistant, Hineko, said. 'It's like no one realises that trying to book your wedding venue with three months to go isn't going to work.'

'They're young and idealistic,' Kelly said, standing up and stretching. 'Not like us bitter hags.' She brandished her phone at them and headed for the door.

'Three divorces and a failed engagement between us,' Hineko called after her. 'You could say we might not be fully qualified for this job.'

Kelly wished she'd put a coat on to call Leah. She had decided to do it in the car park, with the spa hotel she worked at squatting peaceably behind her. She hadn't accounted for the dregs of the spring chill. Leah picked up almost immediately.

'You found it,' she said, straight off the bat.

'What on earth were you thinking?'

'You know Grandma was the reason Dad got out of paying you much in the divorce? I overheard her telling him she'd sort it.'

Kelly had known. Or suspected, anyway.

'I never wanted much anyway, Leah, it didn't matter. We're fine.'

'It's just so unfair.'

'So you thought stealing was the answer? Your father knows.'

'Shit.'

Kelly sank onto a bench. She had thought she'd been steering Leah right. Thought Leah wasn't the kind to care about material wealth.

'I just wanted you to win for once, Mum.'

'Leah, no,' Kelly said, hating the whine in her voice, 'I … I won when I had you.'

'Don't do that. Don't pretend like you don't still love Dad and hate Grandma. I can see it, Mum.'

'We'll talk about how to take this back to your father tonight, OK?'

'Whatever. I don't care.'

Kelly traipsed back to the office, and on the

spur of the moment texted Justin. *I've got the pendant. Can you collect it this evening? Have had the talk with L.*

She'd have to protect Leah from the fallout. After all, she'd only been doing it out of misguided loyalty to Kelly. Sometimes Kelly wished that she could do it all over again. Still have Leah but do things differently with Justin and Evelyn. Maybe there would have been a way of keeping them both on side, of protecting Leah against Evelyn's misogyny. Maybe, even if they'd still got divorced, Kelly could have insisted on joint custody with Leah, instead of taking her refusal to stay with her father as a win.

She was still turning it over in her head when she returned to the office to shrieks of laughter.

'Another one, Kelly! Asking us if we had any spaces this weekend for an elopement!' Hineko told her.

'They're wanting to talk to our manager,' Mark said from the other side of the room. 'We said we'd get you to call them back. I'm guessing they don't think we're able to read a calendar.'

'Ugh!' Kelly said, throwing herself back in her chair. 'I wish all these people would just fuck off. It's not even that nice a building. Have they not seen the carpets?'

'Shhh, you're terrible, Kelly,' Hineko said. On Kelly's breastbone, the monkey's eyes glittered.

———

THE CANCELLATIONS STARTED COMING in that afternoon.

'After consideration, we've decided to postpone …'

'We realised we'd prefer a destination wedding instead …'

'I know what it says in our contract, but could we please get our deposit back?'

Kelly was just beginning to panic in earnest when her dog walker called. 'Sorry to bother you at work, Kelly, but Scribble's not right. I just tried to take him out and he won't come. I think he's sick.'

Kelly was in her car and heading home before the call had ended. Was this karma for Leah's theft? Was it a judgement on Kelly's parenting and life choices? She knew that was ridiculous but she couldn't help but imagine it was the case. They couldn't lose any more bookings for this year without needing to cut staff. That was worrying enough, but Scribble? Had he eaten something he shouldn't have?

The vet couldn't find anything wrong with him

but took blood tests anyway. The dog lay still, his eyes half open, staring accusingly at Kelly from the back of the car on the way home. She had to lift him into the house, and she stayed next to him, as he curled up in his bed and refused to move, until Leah got home from school.

'He won't eat,' she told her daughter as Leah threw down her bag and gathered Scribble in her arms. Another product of Kelly's guilt over the divorce: replace the father with a puppy. God, she'd got things so wrong.

They were trying to get Scribble to drink some water when the doorbell rang. Kelly had almost forgotten that she'd told Justin to pop by.

'I'll face the music,' Leah said grimly.

'No darling, let me deal with it.'

Justin was tight-jawed, strong in a way that he had rarely been in their marriage, and it stirred up feelings that Kelly would rather not be having at the moment. The same raw attraction that had carried them up the altar and to have a child together despite Evelyn's protests.

'I've talked to her about why she shouldn't have done it,' Kelly said, hands out, in between Justin and Leah.

'Why are you acting like I'm a monster?' Justin

said. 'I'm not going to attack my own daughter, for God's sake, Kels.'

'I'm not. I just know that it meant a lot to you and you're understandably angry.'

Leah shot over Kelly's shoulder: 'Maybe if you'd been an actual father and stood up to Grandma occasionally, I wouldn't have done it.'

Justin laughed bitterly. 'You really got into her head, didn't you?'

'Grandma hated me, Dad. Mum was the only one who cared how she made me feel.'

'She didn't hate you, Leah.'

'You're blind then. Fucking blind.'

Justin looked at Kelly. 'So you're letting her swear as well now?'

'She's a young woman, Justin,' Kelly said. 'She sees the truth better than you or me, and she's not afraid to fight over it.'

'You think you didn't fight? All I ever did was try to play middleman to you and Mum.' Justin took another step into the hallway.

'I walked away. I surrendered,' Kelly said. 'I couldn't ever fight for us on my own. You needed to as well, and you chose her.'

Justin stared at her. 'That's really what you think?'

'It's the truth.'

The three of them stood with their regrets, the distance between them cracking like ice. Scribble whined quietly from the other room. Kelly roused herself and drew the necklace out from around her neck. She held it out to Justin.

'Abigail's raging. I think maybe she shouldn't see you for a while, Leah,' Justin said. 'Maybe I can take you out somewhere, just the two of us.'

'Don't bother,' Leah said.

'If either of you had answered your phones, you'd know that she reported the theft to the police this afternoon. I'll try to get them to drop the charges, if I can.'

'You coward,' Kelly breathed, pulling the necklace back. 'You absolute coward. It was Evelyn who caused trouble before and it's Abi now, and you're just a passenger, is that it?'

'No, Kels—'

The anger at seeing her replacement being blamed as the over-reactor, the emotional one, crashed down on Kelly. She might not like Abi much, but she could recognise a woman pushed to extremes when she saw one.

'God, I can't believe I thought you were blameless in all this for so long,' Kelly said. 'If it weren't for Leah I'd wish I'd never met you, Justin.'

The colour drained from Justin's face. His jaw

dropped in horror. 'Kels, no,' he said quietly. 'Kelly, give me the necklace, quickly.'

Kelly stumbled. The ground seemed to lurch again, harder this time. Her vision blurred, her legs gave way.

'Kelly, give me the necklace,' Justin said through fog. Then Leah's arms were around her, and her voice was whispering in her ear, 'Mum? Mummy?'

She blacked out.

SHE CAME to under thick sheets, in a room she didn't recognise. The walls were a horrid shade of green, and the artwork was expensive but tacky.

'Leah?' she called, trying to shift the fog from her brain. Where was she? Was this some kind of hospital? Was it Justin and Abigail's home?

She stumbled down the stairs, passing photographs of children and teenagers she didn't know, dressed neatly in school uniform. There were sounds coming from one of the rooms – the kitchen, she realised, as she followed them and discovered a balding man in his forties and two teenage children sitting at the dining table.

'Good nap?' the man asked.

'What? I'm sorry, but who are you?'

The teenagers snorted, unimpressed. 'Don't be a dick, Mum,' the boy said.

'Darling?' The man stood and pulled her close to him, feeling her forehead. 'Are you all right?'

Kelly looked back to the photographs on the stairway and saw that she was amongst them. A family photo. A wife, a husband and their two kids.

I wish … and Scribble had stopped humping.

I wish … and the clients had fucked off.

I wish … and she had never met Justin.

Kelly ran. She ran out onto a street she didn't know, away from the husband she didn't recognise, and she fell to the pavement and started crying. Crying for the daughter that no longer existed.

HOLLY RACE is an author of young adult books and a Faber Academy graduate. Her fantasy trilogy – *Midnight's Twins*, *A Gathering Midnight* and *A Midnight Dark and Golden* – is set in the world of dreams and nightmares and has been published in English, Spanish and Russian. When she isn't writing, Holly works as a script editor for film and television. She lives in Cambridge with her husband and daughter.

hollyrace.com

ARRIVEDERCI TAKES LONGER THAN GOODBYE

TOM BENJAMIN

D aniel Leicester was crossing Bologna's Piazza Maggiore when, from one of those tables set out in front of the pricey bars, he noticed someone waving. Daniel carried on. No Bolognese he knew would sit there for five euros a coffee – none he would want to stop for at any rate – let alone expose themselves to the relentless July sun, which had almost achieved its zenith.

Yet the man continued to wave – at him, it appeared. Precisely because of that sun there were few others crossing the city's main square, which Daniel himself might have conceded was a sign he remained an outsider to his adopted city – her forty kilometres of porticoes were there for a reason, and during the height of the summer, as with the depths of winter, native Bolognese instinctively stuck to them.

So he drew cautiously, reluctantly, to a halt. The man beckoned him over.

'Danny! *Oh Danny boy* …' Yes, he was singing, a half-finished pint of beer before him. It could only be a fellow Briton – the hillock under the Tottenham Hotspur football shirt, the face that, along with the belly beneath it, had once been flint hard but was now a puffed up, jowl-wobbling public health warning. Daniel wondered if Tommy had done anything about his teeth. '*Oh Danny boy*, I was saying to the missus, that's him – bloody Danny Leicester, as I live and breathe.'

Natalie gave Daniel a grudging nod. Her wine glass was already drained but there was an open bottle of prosecco in the ice bucket. She had not gone to fat like her husband but seemed to have shrunk back, her sunbed-and-cigarette-leathered skin stretched across bone and muscle and silicone. An inadvertent memory from another North London gangster: *'They'll have to hang a Hazard sign on her casket – Not For Cremation – if they want to avoid a chemical incident. Toxic, that one.'*

But it hadn't been Natalie who had gone up in smoke.

'Take a pew, Danny. Wine? Lager?'

Daniel was shaking his head, but the *cameriere* was already hovering beside them. 'I'll have a coffee,' Daniel said in Italian. '*Cappuccio.*'

'Cappuccino,' said the *cameriere*, pointedly ignoring his use of slang and adding in English: 'Chocolate or cinnamon on top?'

'Nothing,' Daniel replied, also in English.

'Get you,' said Tommy. 'Speaking the lingo. But you were always the smart one, weren't you. "Book smart" Chambers used to say. What you doing here, anyway, Danny? Holiday is it? Business?'

Tommy lifted his pint and chucked the rest of

the beer down, his pale blue eyes fixing on Daniel the way hardened criminals did at the moment they were at their most vulnerable – baring their throat.

Tommy raised the empty glass like a trophy. 'I'll have another, José.'

'You know you're in Italy, Tommy,' said Daniel. 'Not Spain.'

'Course he does,' said Natalie.

'At these prices, Danny boy, I'll call him what I fucking want. Anyway, you didn't answer. What you doing here?'

'I live here now, Tommy.'

'Cos you sort of vanished. Well, there was no "sort of" about it, truth be told. When the shit hit the fan, you'd fucked off.'

'Everyone knew I wasn't officially involved,' said Daniel.

'*Officially*,' said Tommy. 'Well, that's one word for it, though honestly I never heard it in the context of trafficking Grade As. The judge didn't let me off for being an "official" drug dealer, like I had a licence, more's the pity.' The *cameriere* arrived with Daniel's coffee – sprinkled, he noted, with chocolate – and Tommy's pint. 'And he didn't give you time at all.'

'As Chambers explained, I was writing about you guys. I wasn't in the business.'

'What part of the business weren't you in though, Danny? Was it the buying? Cos I'm sure I recall you in the backseat when we picked up that consignment from the airfield. Or the partaking, perhaps? You didn't seem shy of a little nose powder yourself.'

'I was there as an observer. You all knew I would be writing about it.'

'That was nuts – typical Chambers! Letting a bleeding journo join our crew. What was it, a film? Thought you'd make a film, did he? Like the Krays? Lock, Stock and bloody Bollocks? How you persuaded him, I don't know. Jesus, crazy times. *Crazy*. He wanted to be a consultant, didn't he? For TV?'

'Something like that.'

'*Yeeeah*. Chambers. He was mad keen on that – always picking holes in films, the telly. "They wouldn't do that, they wouldn't do that". He'd get all worked up. I tell you – he was dead pleased to have met you. Always going on about how we needed to "transition" to legitimate business. Thought he was Michael bleeding Corleone. Didn't see us as criminals – we was working class boys just trying to make our way, that's what he would say.' He raised the fresh pint. '*Chambers*. Here's to him, eh?'

194

Daniel raised his coffee cup. 'What are you doing here, Tommy?'

Tommy chuckled. Daniel noted the teeth – neat, clean, straight and, he understood, entirely false.

'Think I'm on your trail, is that it, Danny?'

'I just wondered if, like you said – you were here on pleasure, or business.'

'Just got out, hasn't he.' Natalie released a spume of tobacco in Daniel's direction. 'Well, he's been out for a bit, but just got his passport back, can travel and whatnot.'

'So that would be "pleasure", Danny Leicester,' said Tommy. 'Venice tomorrow. Natalie's always wanted to see them canals, haven't you love? And Clooney got hitched there – a step up from Walthamstow Registry Office, eh? Then the beach. A friend of a friend has found us a nice spot. Mates' rates.'

'You still with that Italian bird of yours?' asked Natalie. 'Julie, was it?'

'Lucy,' I said. 'That's what Chambers called her, anyway. But it was Lucia.'

'Was?' said Natalie. 'What, she left you?'

'She's dead. An accident.'

'Shame,' said Tommy. 'But you decided to stay. Kids?'

'One.'

'Boy?'

'Girl.'

'I never saw that book, that one what you was supposed to be writing about us.'

'I never wrote it.'

'Never got around to it?'

'Something like that.'

'I never got why it didn't come out. I would have thought it was perfect – you had all the good stuff, and then we got what was coming to us, which the public likes, right? Me three years, Richie nine, poor old Clive-o twelve and Chambers … well he got his noggin blown off. Shame that. I mean, about the book. And of course our boy Chambers would have liked to have lived on, in posterity, so to speak.'

'I never properly understood that,' said Daniel. 'Who killed Chambers. It was always rather … opaque.'

'O-fucking-what?' said Natalie. 'Christ, you and your ponce words.'

'Unclear. They picked you up – Tommy – and Richie, Clive, but Chambers …'

'Crying shame, Danny …'

'I spoke to Inspector Bull; he seemed to think it was a rival mob.'

'He said that, did he? Could've been, Danny.

You know yourself, it's a damn murky world, that's for sure.'

'You must have your suspicions.'

'Must I, Danny? If you say so, I suppose I must.' He drained his pint. 'José! You sure you won't have one, mate? Come on, it's past twelve.'

'I should get going – work.'

'Oh, and what's that, then?'

'You won't believe it.'

'Try me.'

'Private detective.' But Tommy didn't look surprised.

'You always was thick with the Bill – this down to the old man?'

'I'm sorry?'

'Lucy's old man – he was an Italian cop, weren't he?'

'How do you know that?'

The question hung there while others circled like flies. The crew had only met Lucia the once, entirely by accident, when Daniel had accompanied them on a night out and they had bumped into her and her friends in Hoxton High Street. He and Lucia had joined Chambers and one of his girlfriends for a meal, but as much as Lucia might have been charmed by Chambers, she would never have given away her father's past, which back then was cloaked in secrecy – she always said he was a 'civil servant'.

'He was asking, Tommy,' Natalie said flatly, '*how do you know that.*'

'Danny boy here,' Tommy stabbed a stubby finger at Daniel, 'probably thinks because I'm an uneducated, fat ex-con with false choppers I don't know nothing. But that was always his problem, see – he was taken in by Chambers, bought that guff he was the brains, him being such an articulate, dapper fellow. But he got it wrong, that was Danny's prejudice, see – just because I did the heavy lifting and kept shtum didn't mean I was stupid, quite the opposite. Quite the *contrary.*'

'I always saw that, love. That's why I stuck with you, through thick and thin.'

'Or in my case, fat and thin!'

'Oh Tommy, you are a one.' They clinked glasses and looked at Daniel, who was beginning to feel decidedly queasy, as if he was balanced on a ship's rolling deck and had lost sight of the horizon. It only needed Inspector Bull to rock up in a Hawaiian shirt and cargo shorts, maybe even Chambers, clutching his head beneath his arm, to complete the picture.

'So what's your jack, Danny?'

'What do you mean?'

'Story. How did you square it? Moving here?'

Daniel's throat tightened. 'There was Lucia's job. Work drying up at home, the book …'

'"The book?" That must be wearing a bit thin by now.'

'It's all true.'

'I'm sure it is, Danny. You always were very … convincing.'

Another memory: Chambers speechifying some nonsense connecting the international drugs trade to a hotchpotch of outlandish conspiracy theories, but shutting up the moment Tommy – the chiselled, granite Tommy – had shot him a warning look. Daniel saw it now: Tommy, the real brains of the operation behind Chamber's showboating frontman.

'Well.' Daniel lurched to his feet. 'I'd better be getting along.'

'Say hello to Rose for us,' said Natalie.

Daniel froze. 'I never mentioned her name.'

'Didn't you? I'm sure you did, love. Otherwise, how would I have known?'

'She's not a mind reader, Danny,' said Tommy. 'Sure you have to go? What a shame. We was looking forward to some spag-bol. That's what this gaff's famous for, isn't it? You must know a few good places by now, I imagine.'

'Maybe next time,' said Daniel.

'Next time it is, then.' Tommy raised his pint. 'If there *is* a next time.' He winked.

It had been a nasty touch, bringing Rose into it. But Chambers had warned him about Natalie: *toxic*. Yet the couple's point hadn't been to threaten him, Daniel realised.

Tommy and Natalie had taken the trouble to seek him out so he *knew*: that when Daniel had been pulled off the street and confronted with a stark choice by Inspector Bull and the hard men of the Flying Squad to inform on the gang or face a lengthy prison stretch, it had been an artful set up to cover the tracks of the real grass – Tommy.

Daniel had always been amazed at the sheer volume of evidence they had amassed to convict the gang, certainly more than could have conceivably been collected from the conversations he was party to while wearing a wire. But using him as the fall guy had been enough to distract from their real source, who could get off lightly with his reputation intact.

Just three years? Presuming Tommy was out after two for good behaviour, that wasn't bad for access to the ten million the gang had squirrelled away somewhere, leaving the others to dine on prison food and his no doubt dubious assurances.

In the meantime, Daniel's professional and personal life had been left in tatters: he had not only revealed his sources but aided their convictions. Worse, he had betrayed a man he had come to think of as a friend, who had wound up dead under circumstances that were murky to say the least. And, finally, been forced to flee the country after the inspector informed him word had reached them that 'certain arrangements had been made'. Credible or not, it had certainly got him out of the way.

Daniel Leicester had been well and truly played – outsmarted, it was true, by someone he had considered a barely literate, knuckle-dragging thug.

THREE WEEKS LATER, Daniel was sat outside a cheap bar in the shade of a portico when he opened the *Carlino* to see a photo of Tommy and Natalie during leaner, healthier times. In the sun somewhere, probably on holiday in Greece or Spain.

The article told how their yacht had exploded off the coast of Rimini and the couple were feared dead.

No bodies had, as yet, been recovered.

Since **Tom Benjamin**'s Bologna-set mysteries debuted with *A Quiet Death in Italy*, he has received praise from titles including The Times, Daily Mail, Herald Scotland, and Italia! and authors from Harriet Tyce to Ian Moore. His third Daniel Leicester novel, *Requiem in La Rossa*, was published in May 2022, with *Italian Rules* out in 2023.

tombenjamin.com

Twitter: @Tombenjaminsays

Instagram: @Tombenjaminsays

Facebook: @Tombenjaminsays

THE TREE OF SOULS

NYDIA HETHERINGTON

I t was a single flower stem. She might not have seen it, lying forlorn and alone in the shade of the giant yew tree, had there not been a sudden breeze.

Lil McBride dawdled along the old church lane in the village she'd grown up in. Spring was in the air. She could taste it. It had always been her favourite season, back when she was young and knew nothing of life outside the small, closed community she was now back visiting. A fragrant sweetness hit her as she walked, head full of what her mother might want for dinner or what she must do to ensure the daft old bird didn't try to climb up the loft stairs and break her leg, or worse. The smell stopped her in her tracks. She couldn't quite place it, but it was familiar. Enough to give her a jolt and make her halt, take stock of things she could see around her. Only then did she realise where she was, standing by the entrance to the old churchyard. Taken by a whiff of nostalgia perhaps, and aware she probably didn't have the time to do so, Lil pushed the heavy gate open and, like a child entering a secret garden, she stepped inside.

It was an ordinary churchyard, a few hundred years old, she supposed. Lil marvelled at how the smell of fungus and dank vegetation instantly made her memories fly. Then there was that other, sweet, flowery smell that she still couldn't place, almost too heavy for early May. It made the air thick and heady. Whatever the source, it was all part of the smell of her youth – and how it took her back!

When Lil was young, she would come here with Danny Blake. He had been her first love and lived in the big house down at the end of the lane. No one was surprised when they'd got together. Danny and Lil stood out from the other young people of the village. Both almost always dressed in black, donning long sleeves and leather jackets, even on sunny days. Darkly, they'd walk along the lanes and back fields, heads down, long hair covering their faces. She'd felt so proud, with his scissor legs striding beside her. How thin he was, in his black drainpipe jeans and pointed Chelsea boots. Once they'd arrive at the churchyard, their favourite spot for the time they were together, they would spend long afternoons sitting on a fallen log among the graves, reading poetry and wondering about the world and their place in it. It was *their log*. That's what they'd called it. She remembered, then, how keenly she'd felt that ownership, and she couldn't help but feel a pang of regret when she looked at the empty space where the log had been, long since devoured by beetles and woodlice and other crawling things.

Never demonstrative in company, when they were alone Danny would call her his Lily of the Valley. Once, he'd given her two or three blooms of the little white flowers, tiny bells on elegant stems, wrapped in crumpled paper. The sweet stink was so strong she'd gone home with a headache. But she'd never told him. He really wasn't the sort for showy gestures, and she'd been touched, if a little bewildered, by it at the time. The strength of their feelings had been real, though. They were an intense couple and in truth, that was more than a little destructive. Thinking of it, even after so many years, shook her slightly. She pulled her scarf around her shoulders and walked on, weaving her way through the headstones.

The Blakes were what Lil's dad called *an old family*. They'd lived in the village forever, so the young lovers' churchyard walks inevitably took them past the graves and monuments of Danny's ancestors. The stone sarcophagus of his great grandparents' plot, although one of the largest monuments in the cemetery, was plain and weather worn. Still, it looked a proud thing, standing in the shadow of the blackened church. Each time they passed by it, they'd stop. Danny would run his fingers over the words cut deep into the moss-covered stone, blackened by time but still visible, telling of how the old couple had died one year and one month apart, and how they were buried together, in the same hole, side by side. It had seemed romantic, somehow, that death couldn't separate them. At least not for more than one year and one month.

Halting under the yew, Lil leant her back against its enormous, gnarled trunk and felt its deep ridges and rises bite through her thin springtime coat. She closed her eyes for a moment and pictured Danny's face, his silhouette. Then, looking up into the limbs of the tree – *their tree*, of course – she thought she heard his voice. There it was, the guttural laugh, the deep, heavy accent rolling softly through the leaves and branches as they swished and swayed above her. Yet, there was no breeze. The air was as still as the graveyard stones around her.

Lil McBride put her hand on the tree to steady herself. How dry and warm *their* old tree was. How full of life. She imagined she could feel the movement of sap under the thick bark, running in rivulets up and down the trunk, like blood though a vascular system. Then there was the noise, like a pulse or the gentle throb of … what? A heartbeat? What was it the old villagers used to say? That the ancient yew contained the souls of those buried in the churchyard. Lil listened for them now, trapped in the wood, like Ariel in his cloven pine.

A single crow caw followed by the cackle of a magpie knocked her from her reverie, and she almost laughed out loud at herself, standing there like the wide-eyed teenager she'd once been.

The legend of the yew remained thrilling, though. She remembered how much Danny had loved to tell her those stories. Local lore was always so compelling. It seemed to bind them to the place. Like how the tree had survived so many hundreds of years by sucking nourishment from the bones of the dead. With its roots reaching deep down, snaking through the earth, piercing coffins and caskets, splitting them like matchwood so that the tree could imbibe the death vapours of the newly dead, or the rot of those who had been in their graves for many generations, capturing the essence, the very spirits of the people they'd once been.

Who knew how many souls resided in the wood and leaves of the yew, in pain or in peace? Although of a great age, the tree had always been strong and healthy, having thrived, so Danny would say, for who knows how many hundreds or maybe thousands of years on the remains of the village dead. She remembers now, he'd called it The Tree of Souls. Lil and Danny had decided quite early on that this would be their special tree. Not just because of the many days spent sitting beneath its shade, looking up into its branches, describing patterns the shadows made on their faces and telling stories. It was also a connection to Danny's own ancestors. Although his great grandparents' earthly remains lay in a grave on the other side of the church, if the old tales were true, their souls must surely dwell, now and forever, in the yew, like all the dead in the churchyard.

Of course, that was several lifetimes ago now. Lil had moved away when she was still young. How they'd fought when she left. The end of her first love affair had been a tragic mess, so deeply felt and terrible. Remembering it now, almost thirty years on, still made her guts ache. Danny was a gentle young man, really. The memory of his affection for her brought an unexpected smile. Yet, for all that, she'd been cruel at the end. What else could she have done? She couldn't have stayed in the village; she'd needed to spread her wings, to see the world. It was normal at that age. Besides, she had to live the life she'd been living all this time. Strange, after so many years, to think how desperate she'd been to flee to the big city back then, when she'd be ready to do almost anything to leave it now.

I'll stay with you, he'd written in one of his poems

to her. *Forever. I'll put leaves and stones in your hair, sweet Lily of the Valley*. She'd never forgotten that line. He'd read the poem out to her, on the very spot where she was standing now, in the shade of the yew tree. Danny had never left the village; he'd stayed put. As far as she knew he might be down the lane right now, living in his parents' place. They'd lost touch years ago and most of their friends, like Lil, had also moved away. There were no connections anymore. Even Lil's own parents had moved into town a decade ago. She'd only come to the village on an errand for her aging mother. It wasn't somewhere she ever really thought about, and she'd all but forgotten the old churchyard.

Lil sighed as her phone vibrated and croaked in her pocket. She really must change that sound. Her daughter had told her recently that it was a sign of her age, having a frog call as a ringtone. *Only old people do stuff like that*, she'd said. It certainly seemed out of place among the gravestones. Lil McBride took in a lungful of chilled air and looked at her watch. Apparently, this was another sign of being a golden oldie because, her daughter had informed her, no one has a watch anymore. Nevertheless, it did the job, and it was now telling her she really needed to get going. She turned and took a step. That's when she saw the flower.

A slightly wilting lily of the valley lay at her feet. The sickly-sweet smell reminded her why she'd gone into the churchyard in the first place. Of course, she remembered the fragrance all too well now. Lil picked the flower up and frowned. It must be from one of the graves, she thought. But looking ahead she saw another, and then another. There seemed to be a trail of dying flowers laid out before her. Perhaps someone had dropped them. Strange, she thought, how she hadn't seen them earlier. She followed the line of wilting stems, picking them up as she went. The final flower was lying across a stone slab. Feeling a little faint, perhaps because of the smell, or maybe it was the changing spring air turning unexpectedly warm all of a sudden, Lil stopped, knelt down, and placed the flowers she'd collected on the slab. Without thinking, she brushed a light layer of dirt from the gravestone and read the words engraved upon it. It was a simple memorial, nothing fancy.

DANIEL BLAKE

7TH FEBRUARY 1968 – 3RD APRIL 2019

Lil jumped back. Her phone croaked and

buzzed in her pocket. She took it out and tossed it onto the grass beside her. Then she found she was shaking. Her breathing had become shallow and although moments ago she was feeling faint and hot, now she was desperately cold.

Moving forward to get another look at the inscription, Lil heard the leaves of the yew tree sigh behind her. She traced the name on the stone with her finger. It wasn't a mistake. One year and one month ago. The shock made her mouth dry, and she swallowed, hard. Although many years had passed since she'd had any contact with Danny, she felt suddenly untethered. As if the very thing that had been forever rooting her to the Earth had been cut away.

A cloud moved in front of the sun, casting its shadow over the stone, over the village, over Lil McBride, and over every memory and every moment of her lived life. There was a gust of wind, and behind and above her the yew tree began to sway with force, its leaves seeming to sing and then roar her name. But it was his voice she heard, blowing through the branches. *My Lily of the Valley*, it said. *I'll stay with you forever. I'll put leaves and stones in your hair.*

The phone on the ground began to croak and buzz again. But the wind was quite violent now.

Twigs and branches whirled around. Every bit of churchyard detritus was being blown this way and that, hitting Lil where she knelt. She folded her arms over her head and lay down to avoid the full force of the wind in her face. She was lying with her head on the stone slab, on Danny Blake's grave. Her skin was touching his name and the letters seemed to burn into her cheek. She shifted so that her face rested not on the stone, but in the crook of her elbow, and as she did, she felt her greying hair lift into the elements and splay over the gravestone of her first love. Lil turned her face to try and look into the eye of the storm, but all she saw was that her hair was covered in leaves and stones. Then the wind died down as quickly as it came.

The spring sun was bright, and all was quiet in the churchyard. The old yew tree was as still and as silent as the graves it watched over. As usual, the churchyard was empty. Not a single living soul walked the paths between the graves, or knelt before them, heads bent in grief. Only a mobile phone, discarded on a clump of grass, buzzed and croaked like a furious frog, and sprays of wilted lily of the valley lay strewn about the place, as if discarded by a jilted lover.

ORIGINALLY FROM LEEDS, **Nydia Hetherington** moved to London in her twenties to embark on an acting career. Later, she moved to Paris where she ran her own theatre company. Returning to London after almost a decade, she gained a first class honours degree in creative writing. Her debut novel, *A Girl Made of Air*, was published by Quercus in September 2020.

Twitter: @NydiaMadeofAir

Instagram: @nydiamadeofair

waterstones.com/book/9781529408911

SELF-RAISING

CAROLINE BISHOP

Of all the things it could be, it's the lack of self-raising flour that does it. She has scoured the shelves, she has trawled the aisles of this unfamiliar supermarket, and it's not there. She would ask, but she doesn't know what it's called in this language that isn't her own. She would Google it, but her phone is devoid of service down here in this basement Coop. And so she stands in the baking aisle, staring at the place she thinks the self-raising should be, as her eyes prickle and her throat hardens. She blinks rapidly, jabs at her cheeks. *Stupid, stupid, Kate. You are a thirty-year-old woman and it is only flour.*

But it's not.

'It'll be great,' Andy had said when she agreed to move out here to join him. 'I can't wait.' She was excited, too, but the feeling was entwined around many others, not pure and unadulterated like his. But she took the plunge, handing over her belongings to an international transportation company, giving up her beloved flat, abandoning her job, her friends, her family, her life, in order to be with him. The day she arrived they went out for drinks, the local red wine and the grin on his face a dock leaf on the sting of leaving. But the next day, Andy at work, she drifted around his apartment, taking in his furniture, his food in the fridge, his sheets on the bed, and a tightness grew in her chest.

Trailing spouse. She hates that expression. She's not even a spouse. Just trailing, then.

She leaves the supermarket empty handed. She'd only wanted the smell of baking to fill Andy's apartment as it used to fill hers back in London, when she'd invite Sophie round and the two of them would sit on the sofa with prosecco and chocolate sponge, analysing Sophie's bad date or their evil manager's latest demands.

Sophie is her self-raising flour in this new city, this new country: nowhere to be found.

In Andy's apartment she sits, cakeless, with a cup of tea and the post. One letter requests she go to some sort of local government building with her passport, though she doesn't understand why. Another demands she sign a contract for her new health insurance, tying her to a monthly fee that astounds her, jobless as she is. A third comes with a plastic card, welcoming her to the supermarket's loyalty scheme. These letters are the twisting tendrils of a creeper, attaching her to a place that might never let her go.

At 7pm she changes her top, squirts herself with perfume, adds a necklace. Andy said it would do her good, and anyway, he has football practice tonight and she's got nothing better to do, as usual. But as she walks to the bar, dread sloshes in her stomach. Who does this? Who goes online to find friends? Maybe they'll be a bunch of lonely weirdos. Maybe *she's* a lonely weirdo, now.

They are all different nationalities: Alison, a forty-something stay-at-home-mum from Sydney; Stefan, a wiry German postgrad; Christina, a young Austrian marketing manager; and Nora, an unemployed Canadian.

'Kate,' she introduces herself. 'I was a copywriter back home. Here, I don't know yet.'

'Trailing?' Alison asks.

'Yes.' She forces a smile.

'Hard, isn't it?' Nora smiles back.

She nods.

They drink. They talk. Alison shows them pictures of her two kids, Jackson and Olivia. Would it be easier, Kate thinks, if she and Andy had kids? Or would it be even harder, even more of a contrast to her former life? Christina and Stefan pair off, talking in German over white wine on an adjacent table. Alison leaves after a phone call – 'My husband needs me. Jackson won't stop crying' – and then it is just Nora facing her across the table.

'Jeez, I sure hope this gets better,' Nora says, and Kate knows she doesn't mean the evening out.

'I need a job to get a residence permit, but I can't seem to get a job without a permit. So all I do is float around town spending Mark's money and wondering what the hell I'm doing here. Sometimes I think I left myself behind in Vancouver.' She laughs.

'I know exactly what you mean,' Kate says.

'He's worth it, though – Mark, I mean, my fiancé. This job is such a good opportunity for him, he couldn't say no, and we figured, I'm a teacher, I can work anywhere, right?'

'Right.' Kate smiles. She thinks of Sophie, of chocolate sponge and prosecco. 'I loved my job in London,' she says. 'But we're not just our jobs, are we?'

Nora shrugs. 'We're not just trailing spouses either, though, right? I mean, urgh, what a hideous phrase.'

Kate nods. 'Horrific.'

'Fricking awful,' Nora adds, and they both laugh. Christina and Stefan look over and smile, question marks in their faces.

Kate takes a sip of wine. Andy was right, it was good she came out tonight. 'D'you know the worst thing?' she says to Nora. 'I can't find any bloody self-raising flour.' She laughs at herself, but Nora's brow knots.

'Self-raising?'

'You know, flour with raising agent in it.'

'That's a thing? Huh. We don't have that back home, so maybe they don't have it here, either.'

'Really?' She hadn't thought of that. 'So how do you make cakes?'

Nora raises her eyebrows. 'Well, you just add baking powder to plain flour.'

It is so obvious that she is stunned for a moment. *Stupid, stupid* Kate. But this time it's a gentle remonstration, not self-flagellation. And then her stomach begins to shake and she is laughing so hard that water comes to her eyes and slides down her face, for the second time that day.

Nora beams. 'I never realised I was that funny.'

'Listen,' Kate says when she is able. 'Do you want to come over to mine for cake and prosecco sometime?'

CAROLINE BISHOP is the author of two novels, *The Other Daughter* (2021) and *The Lost Chapter* (2022). Following a modern languages degree and a postgraduate diploma in journalism, she was an arts writer in London for many years. She now lives in Switzerland, where she works as a freelance journalist and copywriter alongside writing novels.

carolinebishop.co.uk

Twitter: @calbish

Instagram: @carolinebishopauthor

Facebook: @carolinebishopauthor

AFTERWORD

We do hope you have enjoyed reading the stories in this collection. We have certainly enjoyed writing them. If you would like to spread the word, do tell your friends and, if you have time, consider adding a rating or review for *Unlocked* on Amazon.

If you would like to know more about the D20 Authors and what we get up to, we'd be delighted to connect with you on Twitter: @TheD20Authors.

You can also keep an eye out on Facebook for the various panels and events we run throughout the year. Just search on FB for the Diary of a Debut Novelist group and sign up.

Don't forget to check out all our books on the Bookshop page:

uk.bookshop.org/shop/TheD20Authors

From thrillers to uplit, fantasy to non-fiction, there really is something for everyone on there.

Lastly, thank you so much again for supporting the Trussell Trust by purchasing this anthology. You can find out lots more information about the organisation and its work via its website: trusselltrust.org

Here's to being unlocked.

Philippa East and the D20 Authors

Printed in Great Britain
by Amazon